YOUNG LUTHER

YOUNG LUTHER

THE INTELLECTUAL AND
RELIGIOUS DEVELOPMENT
OF
MARTIN LUTHER
TO 1518

BY

ROBERT HERNDON FIFE

AMS PRESS, INC.
NEW YORK

Reprinted from the edition of 1928, New York
First AMS EDITION published 1970
Manufactured in the United States of America

International Standard Book Number: 0-404-02385-1

Library of Congress Catalog Card Number: 79-131040

AMS PRESS, INC.
NEW YORK, N.Y. 10003

TO

SARAH GILDERSLEEVE FIFE

To conserve space, the Luther editions are abbreviated in citation, as follows:

D. Martin Luthers Werke. Kritische Gesammtausgabe. Weimar, 1883 ff.—*WA.*

D. Martin Luthers sämmtliche Werke. Erlangen, 1827 ff.—*EA.*

Opera latine varii argumenti ad reformationis historiam. Frankfurt und Erlangen, 1865 ff.—*EA, Opp. lat. var. arg.*

Exegetica opera latina. Erlangen, 1829 ff.—*EA, Ex. opp. lat.*

D. Martin Luthers Tischreden. Weimar, 1912 ff.—*TR.*

D. Martin Luthers Briefwechsel, bearbeitet von Enders.—*Enders.*

D. Martin Luthers Briefe, Sendschreiben und Bedenken, hrsg. von W. M. L. de Wette, Berlin, 1825.—*de Wette.*

Luthers Vorlesung über den Römerbrief 1515-1516, hrsg. von Joh. Ficker. Leipzig, 1908.—*Ficker.*

PREFACE

The present work had its origin in a course of lectures on Luther's early religious development delivered at Uppsala University in April, 1927, upon invitation of the Olaus Petri Foundation. At the suggestion of Archbishop Söderblom, President of the Foundation, and with the kind consent of its Directors, the work is published in English. The text has been rewritten and the chapters on Luther's university studies and the final chapter have received some new material.

A portrayal of Luther's religious and intellectual development down to the beginning of the struggle over indulgences is a fascinating task, but by no means an easy one. That it should be undertaken by one who is not a theologian requires some explanation. The studies of Luther upon which the work is based began with no intention of seeking the theological foundations of his career, but were directed toward determining his relation to the literary and humanistic currents of his time. The attempt to sound out the cultural significance of the man from this side led to the sources which record his early conflicts with Scholasticism, and a growing acquaintance with these showed that any study of Luther as educator, translator, fabulist or poet must begin with an understanding of his theological development. Furthermore, as my studies of the Reformation progressed, it became increasingly clear that the whole movement, with its tremendous influence on European culture, must be approached from the standpoint of Luther's break with the scholastic traditions. That this is not the view of many eminent historians, I am well aware, but it is my honest conviction, born out of a study of the sources and growing with an increasing knowledge of these, that the whole conflict which agitated German religious and secular life in the first half of the sixteenth century flowed from one source, the revolutionary changes wrought in Luther's mind in Erfurt and during the early Wittenberg years. Many causes, political, economic and social, contributed their part to the progress of the Reformation, turning its currents now this way, now that, checking its progress or accelerating and intensifying its influence. But to none of these did the movement owe its peculiar nature. It was Luther who set it in motion and gave to it the unique character which persists to the present day.

There is another aspect of Luther's early development which grows in importance and finally becomes of absorbing interest to the student, especially if he be also a teacher. It is the essentially academic character of that development. His conversion came to him while he was a university student. His unrest of soul grew out of severe theological and philosophical studies. His search for new formulas for grace reached a crisis when he came to prepare his first theological lectures. His revolt against the Church developed in the dialectical exercises of the university and was launched as a series of propositions for academic debate. The whole explosive theology was born at a student's desk no less than at a monk's prayer-stool and was nourished to full stature in a professor's classroom.

Luther's early religious development has been traversed by many distinguished pens. It would hardly be possible to add new facts or fresh points of view at the present time. All that I can claim is a methodical and conscientious use of the primary sources and a search for light on them from every competent critic, hostile or apologetic, to whom I had access. Luther's early development has found many interpreters learned in theology, but very few dispassionate ones. His personality still works through his letters, sermons and lectures with powerful vitality to attract or repel. Even though innocent of any conscious bias, the present writer cannot claim to have altogether escaped its influence.

In conclusion it should be said that the following pages are neither a biography nor a chapter in the history of the Reformation, still less a chapter in church history. They are an attempt to show how the personality of Luther was affected by early surroundings and training and to trace as clearly as the sources permit his battle with traditional formulas in theology and philosophy until he found a formula of his own. The limitations of such an inquiry must be acknowledged frankly. Personality is everywhere unique and in its essence unexplainable. All that a work of biographic character can do is to bring its subject into such relief that personality may stand forth with its own peculiar laws and patterns.

Sincere thanks are due to the Directors of the Olaus Petri Foundation and to the authorities of the Uppsala University for many courtesies. I am especially grateful to Archbishop Söderblom for unfailing kindness and helpfulness both in connection with the delivery of the lectures and their publication. Grateful acknowledgments should also be made to the authorities of the libraries at Columbia University and Union Theological Seminary, as well as of the National and the University libraries at Munich. To Dr. Schottenloher, Assistant Librarian at the Bavarian National Library, I am deeply indebted. To Mrs. M. E. Anstensen I owe thanks for help with proofs and index.

CONTENTS

YOUNG LUTHER

I

TRADITION AND EARLY TRAINING

In the year preceding his death Luther sought to trace the history of his early religious life. In a memorable introduction to the first volume of his Latin works he declares that he had once been a stupid Papist, intoxicated, "yes, completely drunken," with the papal doctrine. He represents himself two years after the beginning of the struggle over indulgences, in 1519, as still without confidence that he could give satisfaction to a just and righteous God. Then, after continuous reflection he came to a right understanding of the phrase in Romans i. 17, "for therein is revealed the righteousness of God." [1] The "righteousness of God," *iustitia Dei,* which caused him so much anguish he now interpreted as the *passive* righteousness by which a merciful God makes us just through faith. This discovery that the tormenting *iustitia* means, not the active justice by which God punishes the sinner, but the passive justification

[1] . . . *"nempe iustitia Dei revelatur in illo"* (EA, *Opp. lat. var. arg.,* I, 22).

15

which the sinner receives through faith, made him so happy, he declares, that he felt new-born and seemed to have passed through the open gates into Paradise.

This was not the first time that Luther interpreted his religious experience in terms of the violent and catastrophal. It was his fashion throughout life. In his various accounts of his conversion to the monastic life through a flash of lightning in the forest of Stotternheim, where he appears as a second Paul; in his recollections of his cloister experiences, in which he pictures the soul struggles that well-nigh cost him his life, he reviews his religious development as taking place by a series of active crises. A miraculous light shone around the birth of his religious ideas and their growth appeared as a succession of divine revelations. In retrospect he was conscious only of acute experiences when the finger of God seemed to point the way he should go.

It need hardly be said that the student who seeks to trace the development of Luther's religious ideas cannot be content merely to examine these experiences. The religious thinking of a man so mastered by transcendental conceptions as he was springs from many roots and grows unceasingly through the formative days of youth and early manhood. His religion was a tissue singularly woven together of theological theory and soul experiences. On the basis of tradition taught him so early in life that it had all the validity of an inherited legacy of ideas, he built up by gradual stages out of school, university and cloister studies and out of his experiences as a monk and monastic administrator, as scholar and as teacher, a complex of faith which eventually made him independent of teachers and books. To the student who seeks to piece it together the story of such a development must reveal itself as very different from the experiences as recalled by the hero of them. What appeared to Luther as a series of sudden illuminations presents itself to the historian of his life as a succession of imperceptible steps, and the crises which he describes so dramatically seem to his biographer but registrations of completed processes.

Indeed, one can go further and in the light of documents which we have and by the use of methods commonly employed in historical inquiry note important phases in this development which were not apparent to Luther himself. Thus the lectures on the Epistle to the Romans of 1515-16 reveal a state of thought as regards evils in the Church and the position of the Pope and Council which Luther does not formally record until two years later, when the hearing before the papal envoy Cajetanus at Augsburg showed him the width of the breach which already separated him from the traditional system. Similarly the great disputation with Eck in 1519 reveals to the student—though Luther himself does not seem to have realized it at the time—that he had come far in the denial of the right of the Pope to rule in matters of faith and in the refusal to recognize the authority of the Council over the individual conscience.

Naturally the sources do not permit anything like a complete picture of Luther's religious development, nor could such a picture be drawn even if we were in possession of a much richer mass of source material than we have. The processes by which a thoughtful man adjusts himself to tradition, to lessons from teachers and books, to social and cultural environment and life's many experiences are far too complex for analysis and for the most part quite withdrawn from study or observation. All we can do is to array these elements and seek to mark off in rough outline the stages of inner growth. In Luther's case we are aided by the fact that the development which we have to trace was a subject of keen interest on his part throughout life and called forth frequent memories and observations in speech and writing. The attempt to evaluate these recollections properly and with the help of all other available sources to trace the genesis and growth of his religious ideas to maturity is a fascinating but difficult problem in historical method. The highly subjective character of Luther's statements regarding all that concerned the days in the monastery, the unreliability of the transmission to posterity of a considerable part of his recollections, the pitfalls prepared by the critics and apologists of four polemical centuries during which Luther has been the object of attack and defense—all these add to the difficulties of the investigator. The greatest difficulty is of course within himself, the tendency for which Goethe's Faust scores his pedantic famulus Wagner, the tendency to interpret the psychology of the stormy decades which preceded the Reformation in terms of our own time and to create out of Luther's development an ideology which must reflect chiefly the limitations and prejudices of the investigator. The dynamic force of Luther's temperament even after the lapse of four centuries is so powerful that the student finds himself ever in danger of being warped out of a judicial attitude toward the sources.

The sources on which a knowledge of the early religious development of Luther depends, like all sources pertaining to his life, flow richly, far too richly indeed for one lifetime to master them all properly. Here the labor of many scholars has gone before; and especially in the last two decades, after the critical work of Heinrich Denifle [2] had spurred German apologists to renewed activity, much has been made available in accurate and scholarly form which was formerly difficult of access or existed only in uncritical and unreliable texts. In the main, the primary sources necessary to mark the chief steps in Luther's religious and theological development are

[2] *Luther und das Luthertum,* 1. Ausg., Mainz, 1904.

now open to the student. These are, first, his letters
and the contemporary reports and documents which
he prepared in connection with the hearing before
Cajetanus at Augsburg [3] and the conferences with
Karl von Miltitz; second, his early marginal notes and
his exegetical lecture courses on the Psalms and Romans and, though less important, on Galatians; third,
the memoranda and records of his disputations and
those which he inspired on the part of his students;
and fourth, his controversial articles and treatises
from middle life, and his prefaces. Furthermore,
many references by Luther in his sermons and *Table
Talk* in later years throw light on earlier experiences.
These records were noted down and transcribed by
his students and associates and are frequently colored
by faulty tradition and by the partisanship of scribe
and apologist. At best they represent the recollections of Luther expressed without formality or re-
serve from ten to thirty years after the event. In
addition to these there are letters and recollections of
contemporaries which are of value, even though
strongly colored by partisan bias. All in all, the
sources are sufficient to set forth, at least in outline,
the history of the struggle of a soul, possessed of the
God-idea as few have been, to attain peace within an
inherited and traditional framework, and, failing
that, to find paths which should lead out of tradition
into independence. They mark the stages of an in-

---

[3] Published in the fall of 1518 as *Acta Augustana* (*WA*, II, 1ff.).

cessant combat by one to whom combat was an essential part of life.

Luther regarded the development of his religious thought as practically completed in 1519.[4] We shall find ourselves obliged to set the date a year or more earlier. In 1518, when he came forth from the university to carry into the outside world the ideas of the impotence of the will of man, of sin and the method of obtaining grace, which he had been slowly maturing in cell and lecture room, his struggle with religious dogma was already at an end. Minor readjustments followed and many soul experiences of a bitter sort rocked the structure of his faith, but at no time thereafter was the basis of his system of religious thought endangered. It but remained for him to draw the consequences as they concerned the political and social problems of his time and the relation of the individual to the church and to the community of believers. This he did in the three great tractates of 1520: the address *To the Christian Nobility of Germany, On the Freedom of a Christian,* and *On the Babylonian Captivity of the Church.*[5]

The social and cultural background upon which Luther came into the world was that of the Thurin-

---

[4] *Praefatio* of 1545 (EA, Opp. lat. var. arg., I., 22ff.).

[5] The revised course of lectures on Galatians, published in 1519, contains definite and formal expression of the assurance of salvation for the believer, a stage of faith which Luther had not yet reached in the lectures on Romans in 1516. Indications that he had already reached it in 1518 are, however, to be found in his Hebrews course of that year. Cf. below, p. 216.

gian family, half peasant and half town-dweller, at the end of the Middle Ages. On the canvas of Lucas Cranach we may still see the parents, Hans and Margareta Luther, as they looked in later middle life, with the broad, low brow and the toil-hardened features that mark the half-rural townfolk of northwestern Thuringia to the present day. Friend and foe of the son have seen to it that bright lights and heavy shadows should fall on the character of Luther's parents. Rejecting all hearsay and tendencious evidence, we are justified by reliable sources in regarding the Luther household as a normal one, conforming to the moral and religious standards of a North German family of its station. The father was undoubtedly headstrong and violent, but practical in his nature and earnest and steady of purpose. Both parents appear to have treated their children with the severe discipline that belonged to the spirit of the age, an age that held the rod to be inseparable from all education and carried every form of punishment to the point of brutality. Luther's life-long respect for authority in temporal affairs, his entry into the cloister and his ready fulfillment of the duties there point to the advantages of a stern education for a youth of a naturally violent temperament and a naturally obstinate will. The position of trust which the community twice bestowed on Hans Luther, membership in the Mansfeld "Commission of Four," a committee of burghers charged with the duty of representing the citizens in the transactions of the municipal council;[6] the friendship of Luther's friends and of the clergy and teachers in Mansfeld; the generous affection with which the elder Luther followed his son's studies; and finally, the respect with which Martin always speaks of his father, all point to a character of moral earnestness on the part of the parent. The traditional superstitions of the father were evidently tempered by sound, practical sense, for he strongly opposed his son's entry into the monastery, and when Martin related to him the vision in the forest near Erfurt which caused him to utter the vow to become a monk, the older man exclaimed, "Supposing it was an evil spirit!"[7] That the elder Luther cultivated something more than the traditional usages of generosity toward the church is underscored by his son, who remembered many years later that his father brought a gift of twenty florins to the Augustinians on the occasion of his first mass, although he was opposed to Martin's investiture.[8]

In comparison with the vigorous outline which the sources draw of the father, Luther's mother, Margareta Ziegler, presents a very incomplete and pale picture. Luther's friends mention the respect in which the town held her, and their testimony and Luther's own leave the impression that she was indus-

[6] From 1491 on; cf. Krumhaar, *Versuch einer Geschichte von Schloss und Stadt Mansfeld*, 1869, 25ff.

[7] *De votis monasticis* (*WA*, VIII, 574 [1521]).

[8] *TR*, II, 1558.

trious, self-denying and devout. The interest of scribe and apologist in that stern era did not linger on female characterization.

In addition to the blessings of poverty and stern discipline and the example of iron industry and courageous enterprise, Luther received from his parents and home a fund of mythological lore, to which he added richly by reading and association. "Superstition is in-born in energetic and powerful natures," declares Goethe. A family which like the Luthers stood on the dividing line between peasant and burgher borrowed superstitions from sources open to both of these classes. As hard work and thrift were the mainsprings of their outer life, so superstition and faith intertwined and merged to make up the inner furniture of the mind. How completely the boy absorbed the mythology which surrounded his childhood may be seen in the sermons and *Table Talk*, where evidence meets us constantly of his persistent belief in the creations of the lower mythology of the German peasant. Upon this he built in later years a complex structure of superstitions derived from scholarly sources. It was the early mythology, however, gathered from family and community, which set its stamp so strongly on young Luther's life that in reviewing his later references to the creatures of German mythical fancy one cannot avoid the conviction that he lived in childhood in a milieu which, even measured by the standards of the later Middle

Ages, was unusually imaginative and superstitious. After the study of Aristotle's *Physics* at the university and the reading of a respectable list of classical authors, and after many years of association with men of humanistic training, he still at fifty years of age retained unshaken his belief in the whole formidable system of popular mythological figures. Only a fancy abnormally sensitive to the other-worldly and from childhood upwards highly stimulated by fear could have peopled house and forest, field and stream, earth and air and water with so many creatures of harmful character.

The interest in the nimbus of superstition which gathers around Luther's person began very early in his career and has continued active down to the present day. As early as 1580 Wilhelm Lindanus relates that the Emperor Charles V saw a devil on Luther's shoulders in Augsburg in 1518! [9] This interest is due in part to the very colorful manner in which Luther himself puts before us the world of devil and witch, of nixie and cobold, which formed the texture of his faith. It is trite to say that he shared here in great part the faith of his contemporaries. The point to be determined is how far he departed from the norms of his time and whether his myth-creative nature led him to alter the symbols and patterns of the period. It is well known that, as the fifteenth century approached its end, a great number of popular superstitions found

[9] E. Klingner, *Luther und der deutsche Volksaberglaube*, 1912, 29 Anm.

their way into the sermons of the clergy and the papal bulls. In preachers like the Strassburg satirist, Geiler von Keisersberg, in Humanists like Johannes von Tritheim, in works like the *Malleus Maleficarum,* in the canonical law itself we find a mass of material mingled of popular superstition, distorted classical stories and tales of international currency. A rich demonology, made up of Christian-Germanic creations and Germanic transmutations of heathen gods, was a part of current faith. Pacts with the devil were generally accepted as true. Magicians traveled back and forth in Germany: Melanchthon's contact with the magician Faust in after years is related by his students. Witches occupied the mind of peasant and scholar alike, although not so exclusively as a century later.[10]

In the acceptance of this world of magic Luther was aided by an emotional temperament and a colorful imagination. Many of the pictures that he draws rest, to be sure, on the highest theological authority. First of all, the Bible itself in such accounts as those of the temptations of Christ and of Paul supplied material for his demonology. Paul warns the Corinthians against evil spirits; both Peter and Paul declare certain phenomena which we regard as the result of natural laws to be the work of demons. In such passages as these as well as in Augustine and the canon

[10] Klingner, *op. cit.,* p. 5, Anm. 1, for authorities on demonology of the period.

law young Luther found forms and models for the anthropomorphic conception of the devil and the vivid demonology which are such important elements of his faith.

From these periods of his life we are able to form a general idea of the world of lower spirits as Luther conceived it. It appears in one of his early sermons, that on the Ten Commandments, delivered in 1516 (published 1518); [11] in various conversations after 1531, included in the *Table Talk*, and in the Commentary on Genesis,[12] in 1541. So far as a comparison of these sources is possible, it shows no change throughout life in his views or pictures of the world of baleful spirits.[13] At all periods he paints them with extraordinary intimacy and a vivid picturesqueness which is frequently touched by a lively humor. The pictures which he draws of the devil are so colorful and definite that they suggest such childhood associations and early fixations of ideas as might have originated in the devil figures in Shrovetide plays or in similar dramatic exhibitions given at annual fairs in the North German towns. The devil plays the harp; he goes to a dance; he sits in the corner behind the great oven and mocks at us. He appears as a dandy, wearing a green hat with a blue feather.

[11] *Decem praecepta Wittenbergensi praedicata populo* (*WA*, I, 401ff.); cf. the interesting notes by Kawerau in Luther's *Ausgewählte Werke*, *Volksausgabe* (IV, 1, 41ff.).

[12] *WA*, XLII.

[13] Cf. Klingner, *op. cit.*, 17.

He shows himself in countless forms: as a priest, as a monk, in the pulpit, as the cellarer in a monastery. He sends all evil upon us—storms, hail, poisonous air; he ruins crops and causes animals to fall sick. He falls organically into the soul struggles in the cloister and reappears constantly during later crises. In Luther's accounts of these he seems to be a sort of personification or realistic symbol of theological error. Thus, in the Wittenberg convent at a time when the young professor is struggling with the dogma of justification in preparing his first lectures on Psalms, the devil disturbs him with noises in the refectory. In the tense days of the journey to the Diet of Worms he sends the traveler an illness.

In mature years Luther dips constantly into the reservoir of childhood tradition and fancy, and peoples stream, field and forest with harmful demons. Pictures of this kind appear in lectures, sermons and conversations clear down to old age. "In my home neighborhood," he tells his table companions, "on a high mountain called the Poltersberg there is a lake. If one throws a stone into it, there comes up a great storm and the whole country around is stirred and moved by it. Therein dwell devils who are held prisoners there." [14] At forty-three years of age he declares his belief that demons in female form are to be found in a pond behind the Probstei in Wittenberg:

[14] *TR*, III, 3841-1538.

"yes, without doubt it is quite full of them." [15]
Nixies dwell in the river Elbe and draw men down
to death.[16]   Prussia is quite full of devils.[17]

In the world of spirits that surrounded the eager
mind of the growing lad witches must have played
an important rôle.   In later years he recalls that they
cast their spells over field, man and beast.[18]   Boys
were their especial victims and one of his brothers
succumbed to their magic.[19]   The growing crops
were at their mercy and even the clergy were help-
less against their attacks.   His mother was tormented
by them and was obliged to propitiate their favor,
"for they sent pains upon her children until they
cried like death."[20]   As he held retrospect over the
matter in later years, it seemed to him indeed that
witches had been especially active in his childhood.[21]
He himself had seen many victims and he retained
through life a great hatred for them.   From his
childhood he retained the belief that sickness was
caused by demons who defied the physicians.[22]   Nature
swarmed, in fact, with beings of potential harmful-
ness.   The cobold might infest the house.   Men were
lured to an evil fate by Dame Hulda, a seductive
Germanic goddess of beauty whose cult was especially active in Luther's part of the country.[23]   The

[15] WA, XX, 292.
[16] WA, XXIX, 401 (1529).
[17] TR, III, 3841.
[18] WA, XL, 2, 112.
[19] WA, XL, 1, 315.

[20] TR, III, 2982b-1533.
[21] WA, XL, 1, 313.
[22] TR, II, 2267b-1531.
[23] WA, I, 406.

incubus and succubus begot with human beings demoniacal children.[24]   Evil spirits might substitute for a child in the cradle a horrible changeling of diabolical origin.[25]

These traditions which Luther absorbed during childhood were singularly persistent throughout his life; nevertheless the respect for written sources which the student and professor drew from his studies and from association with Humanists was not altogether without effect on Luther's mythology. We find here and there a tendency to test his demonology by the Scriptures, and he is thus led at times to discard superstitions which were common to his age. The miraculous deeds of magic related by such distinguished Humanists as Johannes Tritheim and Melanchthon were contemptuously rejected by Luther as delusions of the devil. He would have nothing to do with the magic mirror or the divining rod.   Crystal gazing he held to be a delusion and love-philters a cheat.   He did not believe in the ability of witches to voyage through the air to conventicles nor in the return of the dead, and he was very critical of dreams and omens, which he held to be evidences of God's anger and boding no harm to Christians.[26] Comets and other celestial wonders are meant as threats to the godless, not to the pious, "for they do

[24] WA, I, 407, 410; TR, III, 3676; cf. EA, Ex. opp. lat., II, 127.

[25] TR, IV, 4513-1539; V, 5207; cf. WA, XIV, 185.

[26] Klingner, op. cit., 96.

not need them." [27] In spite of the arguments of Melanchthon and the almost universal opinion of the age, he held astrology to be a fake. None of these things was to be found in the Bible. It was also a literal interpretation of the Bible which prevented his acceptance of Copernicus' theory of the universe; nor would it permit him to believe that the planets received their light from the sun. He must have been obliged to defend his conservatism in this regard many times in the Wittenberg circle, where these theories apparently were viewed with sympathy. Through Melanchthon in 1535 Copernicus' favorite scholar, Joachim Rheticus, established himself there.[28]

In a family and environment like that into which the boy was born religion must have played an important rôle, which went beyond mere exterior observances. Legal documents for the county and city of Mansfeld in the last quarter of the fifteenth century [29] show a vigorous religious life during the years of Luther's boyhood, but do not indicate that there was anything abnormal in it or that the neighborhood was a stage for any of the heresies or reform movements so common in other parts of Germany in the second half of the fifteenth century. The county of Mansfeld contained in Luther's childhood almost a

[27] *Vorrede zu Lichtenbergs Weissagung* (WA, XXIII, 10 [1527]).

[28] Cf. Klingner, *op. cit.*, 101, Anm. 4. Melanchthon published in 1535 a work defending astrology as a science.

[29] Reprinted by Krumhaar, *op. cit.*, 24ff.

dozen cloisters well furnished with holy relics and popular objects of pilgrimage. Luther recalled in later years picturesque features of local religious life, such as the pealing of the chapel bell of St. Cyriac at Wimmelburg which was supposed to heal one possessed of the devil.[30] Within the city the liberal donations to religious objects, so characteristic of Germany in the later fifteenth century, provided constantly for soul masses or founded additional altars in the church of St. George with rich stores of indulgences.[31] As a boy young Martin may have participated in church and school in the beautiful liturgical forms of service of the later Middle Ages, with the choral and communal singing that especially marked the German churches. As a schoolboy he would have been especially called upon for the musical service of the choir at matins, mass and vespers.[32] He would have marched in solemn procession and joined with his comrades in the festive services which, with their rich liturgy of psalm and prayer, with collect and responsory and antiphony, kept step with the measured revolution of the Christian year.

That this must have had an abiding influence on a boy of deeply emotional nature and unusual musical gifts is obvious. His fancy was constantly occupied with the brilliant figures of Christian mythology. In

[30] *TR*, I, 830. Luther ridicules the superstition as "*Wahn und Irrtum.*"

[32] Krumhaar, *op. cit.*, 23 ff.

[33] Krumhaar, *op. cit.*, 29.

later years he complained that his childhood had known only the severe character of Christ: "I was so accustomed from childhood up that I must turn pale and take fright when I heard the name of Christ called, for I was not otherwise instructed than to hold Him for a severe and angry judge." [33] He turned, he tells us, to the gentle Virgin and the saints for intercession with the severe judge upon the throne.[34] Undoubtedly we have here some coloring from a later polemical standpoint. But there is reason to believe that as a boy he accepted with the traditional piety of family and community and absorbed with active imagination the polytheism of the medieval masses. It must have been in childhood that the habit of honoring the saints became so fixed that it was with great reluctance that he surrendered it in later years, long after other usages and dogmas of the church had been discarded. While the reform ideas were germinating in him in 1516 he admitted whole-heartedly the worship of saints and the intercession of a particular saint, although he insisted that aid should be solicited for spiritual rather than temporal blessings; [35] and as late as 1519, when girding himself for the contest with the apologists of the papacy, he proclaimed his faith in the performance of miracles

[33] *EA*, I, 261.

[34] *WA*, XLV, 86 (1537).

[35] "*Nec prohibeo sanctos invocari pro temporalibus, sed quod solum pro temporalibus id faciant damno, neglectis eorum virtutibus et exemplis*" (*WA*, I, 417).

beside the holy bodies and graves of the saints. [36] His imagination must have been captivated by the picturesque saint-cults, which multiplied and became more and more specialized toward the end of the Middle Ages. In place of Christ, the severe judge, his affection would turn toward St. George, the dragon slayer, the patron of the principal church in Mansfeld, or to St. Anne, to whom the miners of the neighborhood looked for protection and wealth.[37] In the fateful two years between the lectures on the Epistle to the Romans and the Leipsic disputation we find him now and again making an effort to free himself from the ban of the still-venerated figures of Christian mythology; and as late as 1530 in the *Sendbrief vom Dolmetschen* he declares: "It has been beyond all measure difficult for me to tear myself loose from the saints, for I have been immeasurably deep in them and over my head in them." [38] Religion and superstition melted together indistinguishably in the mind of the adolescent boy as they did in the minds of the perpetually adolescent masses around him. His soul life must have become as colorful as that which the artistic fancy of his age records on the windows of the late Gothic churches of north German cities. The baleful forms which filled

[36] *Unterricht auf etliche Artikel* (WA, II, 69ff.).

[37] Cf. E. Schaumkell, *Der Kultus der heiligen Anna am Ausgang des Mittelalters*, 1893, 13ff.; cf. WA, I, 415. The cult of St. Anne developed with great rapidity in Luther's boyhood.

[38] *WA*, XXX, 2, 644.

house, field and forest with evil spirits were neutralized and restrained in the mind of the growing lad by the loving interposition of the angels and sainted men and women who dwelt in the vestibule of divine power.

The first steps in his regular religious instruction were undoubtedly taken in the Mansfeld school. Hither, Luther recalls many years later, he was carried as a *pusille,* or child.[39] This was in all probability one of those municipal Latin schools which had become the basic educational institutions in the German cities. As a type it enjoyed the especial care of the city council, which at that time exercised a sharp control over school life, as is attested by the records of many South German cities. The controlling hand of the council made itself felt especially in checking a too vigorous punishment of the pupils, which in accordance with the spirit of the time took many cruel forms. Luther's arraignment of the Latin schools a quarter of a century later in his address *To the Councillors of all German Cities* as "devourers and destroyers of children" attacked especially the crude forms of discipline which they cultivated as a part of a general narrowness of program and inefficiency.[40] There is no means of knowing whether the Mansfeld school was better or worse than the other

---

[39] *de Wette,* V, 709-1544. The boy who carried him was Nicholas Omeler, who afterwards married into the Luther family. Cf. Krumhaar, *op. cit.,* 31.

[40] *WA,* XV, 27ff.

"Trivial" schools of the day. In some respects, at least, it cannot have deserved the attacks which Luther makes upon its type later, for here he must have laid the foundation for the study of Latin, which formed in one way or another the whole subject matter of the school program [41] and in which he afterwards attained the command of so highly individual a style.

In the first *fibula* or reader to which he was introduced he found the primary formulas of Christianity: the Ten Commandments, the Apostles' Creed, the prayers and sacraments. It is hardly probable that he himself had a book in his hand until some years later, for little Thomas Platter, a Swiss schoolboy who wandered north to the humanistic schools at Naumburg and Breslau at the end of the first decade of the sixteenth century, still found no school books in many classes.[42] The teachers dictated and explained the forms; the scholars repeated, wrote down and memorized. The materials of school study were of moral rather than directly religious character. Aside from the grammar of Donatus, they comprised the Distiches of Cato, selections from Aesop's fables and from Boethius; and possibly Plautus and Terence may have contributed material.

Music doubtless formed an essential part of the program—a matter of importance, for Luther's

[41] *WA*, XV, 38.

[42] Gustav Freytag, *Bilder aus der deutschen Vergangenheit*, II, 2.

musical genius must have budded early. The contents of the songs must have been in considerable part
religious. An abiding memory of Luther's childhood
was one of singing on the streets of Mansfeld, probably the folksongs which were sung from house to
house at Christmas and other church festivals.[43] A
great deal of religious instruction in Germany was
carried on through singing, which in its complex
liturgical forms had become a difficult art even before
the Renaissance brought a more highly diversified
technique from Italy. The services of the schoolboys
required daily religious exercises; as choir boys they
played an especially important rôle in the processions
and religious festivals which were such a passion of
the later Middle Ages and which allowed so much
opportunity for musical features. So ardent a spirit
as young Luther's not only received the training in
musical technique which these observances brought
and which was later so important for him, but also
must have stored within itself many of the phrases
and pictures which later came so readily to hand from
the solemn litany of later medieval worship as sung
in psalm and hymn, in versicle and responsory.

The drill in religious formulas and the practice in
liturgical forms went hand in hand with other instruction, as the boy mounted the scale of studies
through the *Trivium* of grammar, logic and rhetoric.
In Magdeburg, whither he went in his fourteenth

[43] *TR*, I, 137.

year in accordance with the wandering customs of medieval schoolboy life, he came into contact with a religious group which cannot have been without influence on his development, even though his stay in the Elbe city was only for a year. These were the Brethren of the Common Life, *Nullbrüder,* as Luther calls them in recounting his association with the school twenty-five years later.[44] The transfer to the school at Magdeburg was in accordance with the usages of the Middle Ages and Renaissance, and no great adventure; and the fact that he "went after bread and sang for bread in God's name," as related by a contemporary biographer, Mathesius, and confirmed by Luther himself for the Eisenach period,[45] was quite in accord with the habit of a time which was wont to support education in part by doles to singing scholars. Magdeburg itself was the seat of an archbishop and the site of a great cathedral with forty altars and a rich store of relics; [46] and at the house of the Brethren of the Common Life, which lay close to the cathedral, the schoolboy was in the shadow of a great complex of churches, cloisters, chapter-houses and episcopal buildings, a typical medieval setting for the schooling of a future cleric.[47]

[44] Letter to Claus Sturm, June 15, 1522 (*EA,* LIII, 137).

[45] *"Ich bin auch ein solcher parteken hengst gewest und hab das brot für den heusern genomen, sonderlich zu Eisenach jnn meiner lieben stad"* (*WA,* XXX, 2, 576).

[46] Cf. G. Hertel in the *Geschichtsblätter für Stadt und Land Magdeburg,* XXXVII, 1, 1902, 163 ff.

[47] F. W. Hoffmann, *Geschichte d. Stadt Magdeburg,* 1845, I, 437 ff.

With the Brethren of the Common Life the boy came into contact with an order which combined the mystic enthusiasm of the full Middle Ages with an active mission of physical and moral helpfulness. The *devotio moderna,* as interpreted by the founder of the order, Gerhard Groote of Deventer, expressed the social tendencies of later medieval mysticism. Along with a profound devotional life, cultivated in common and in close affiliation with various monastic orders, especially the Augustinians in Holland and North Germany, the Brethren of the Common Life lived according to the three major monastic rules of St. Benedict—poverty, chastity and obedience— dwelling together and holding property in common. They were not mendicants and they avoided the ascetic exercises of the mendicant orders. Rather they devoted themselves to teaching and to caring for boys, and in the later fifteenth century to reformatory efforts in education.

The mystical writers of the Brethren of the Common Life were later to exercise a not unimportant in- fluence on Luther during his struggles to find a new formula for justification. He evidently knew and was influenced by the spiritual exercises of their great soul-physician, Gert Zerbolt, during the preparation of his first course of lectures on the Psalms,[48] and in the lectures on Romans he pays a ringing tribute to the description of sin in a devotional tractate by this

[48] *WA,* III, 648.

author, which he erroneously ascribes to the founder of the order, Gerhard Groote of Zutphen.[49] In 1522 he calls attention to the remarkable similarity between his reformatory ideas and those of another member of the Deventer house, Wessel Gansfort. It is of interest that in his fifteenth year he came under the influence of this group of practical mystics, whose great schools at Deventer and Zwolle had for a century been sending boys out into the religious life of the Netherlands and Germany. The schools of the order in Münster in Westphalia and Schlettstadt in Alsace were gateways through which pre-humanistic school reforms found their way eastward and must have made their influence felt in the Magdeburg region.

The establishment of the Brethren of the Common Life in Magdeburg had been in existence for several years when Luther came there.[50] Whether they maintained a school there as at Zwolle and Deventer in Holland and elsewhere is uncertain. Their mission of bringing more religion into the schools, thereby making a knowledge of the Bible and the use of the vernacular in religious service more

---

[49] "I have nowhere found a more faithful description of original sin than in the treatise 'Beatus vir' of Gerhard Groote, who did not speak like a bold philosopher but like a good theologian" (Ficker, 2, 145, 3). The reference is to Zerbolt's Devotus tractatulus de spiritualibus ascensionibus; cf. Hyma, The Devotio Moderna, Ann Arbor, 220ff. Luther's relation to the devotional works of the Deventer group is not altogether clear and deserves further study.

[50] It was probably established in 1489. Cf. Hoffmann, op. cit. 437.

widespread, was accomplished in many places from outside of school walls. Their influence bore upon the physical and moral welfare of the boys, who might be poor scholars, or like Martin Luther, not without means and protection. As a resident in their house he must have been exposed constantly to the devotional exercises which here as at Zwolle and elsewhere accompanied the "collations" of the schoolboys. Here the boy might see close at hand a careful observance of private devotional and liturgical exercises, for the brothers kept the round of monastic religious observances, and the cultivation of religious zeal by means of the careful notation of spiritual progress and the regular reading of the Scriptures. Coupled with these were deeds of practical human service within and without the house. Thirty-eight years later, in a letter to the Council of Herford, Luther speaks of the order with enthusiasm as a witness of Christian freedom and the apostolic life.[51]

In daily contact with a group of deeply pious men the growing boy became acquainted with the magic of self-sacrifice and the mystic lure of the yoke of God. His mind was furnished with vivid and ineffaceable impressions of the inner charm as well as the pomp and majesty of the religious life. One of these pictures recurred to him in later years as a classic type of ascetic devotion. He recalls having seen on the Broad Street of the city a Prince of Anhalt, a

[51] October 24, 1534 (EA, LV, 66).

brother of the Bishop of Merseburg, bent under a heavy sack of bread which he had begged for his cloister. "So had he fasted, watched and chastised himself that he looked like a Death's head, nothing but skin and bone. He died then soon afterwards, for he was not able to endure such a hard life." [52]

[52] *Verantwortung der aufgelegten Aufruhr* (WA, XXXVIII, 105); cf. TR, VI, 6859.

II

SCHOOL AND UNIVERSITY

It has been pointed out that the surroundings of Luther's boyhood were such as to cultivate in normal fashion the religious ideas current in the North German towns in the last quarter of the fifteenth century. Nothing in his own statements regarding his early life, either uttered directly or through the mouth of his contemporary biographers, nothing in the sources pertaining to the Mansfeld and Magdeburg regions, points to physical, moral or religious conditions different from those which might have surrounded any boy of a North German city who was equipped with the modest means which the middle-class family of the day was accustomed to regard as sufficient assistance to give to the son who was seeking an education.

The unusual circumstances which the early biographers threw about the boyhood of Luther disappear on close scrutiny. The extreme poverty of the parents to which he refers in later years cannot have lasted beyond early childhood.[1] The ardent tempera-

[1] *"Parens meus in adolescentia sua ist er ein armer hewr gewesen. Die mutter hatt all yhr holtz auff den rucken eingetragen. Alsso haben sie uns erzogen"* (TR, III, 2888a-1533).

ment of the father, which is touched with humor in
the picture which the son draws of him, was a family
trait.[2] It did not affect the elder Luther's standing
in the community, nor the respect in which he was
held by the clergy of his native place and by Luther's
friends,[3] nor the deep affection which the son had
for him.[4] The cruel punishment inflicted on him by
his mother, which is the one memory which Luther
records of the character of that parent, and by his
schoolmasters, was too much in accord with the
savage disciplinary customs of the later Middle Ages
to be regarded as exceptional. Luther's statements
on this subject are quite definite and well authenticated. He criticizes his parents and teachers for
severe punishments—"although they meant it for the
best"—and for failing to understand the temperament of children. He declares that he was beaten in
school fifteen times in one morning and that his parents punished him brutally for trifling causes, and he
ascribes to this a timidity which finally brought him

[2] *"Reliqui ebrii sunt laeti et suaves, ut pater meus, cantant, iocantur"* (*TR*,
IV, 5050-1540). The remark was made in reproving a drunken nephew, Hans
Polner, who was for thirteen years in Wittenberg. Cf. *Enders*, VIII, 188,
Anm. 4.

[3] Schlüsselberg, *Oratio de vita et morte Lutheri*, Rostock, 1610; cf.
Melanchthon, *Corpus Reformatorum*, VI, 156.

[4] Cf. the introduction to *De votis monasticis* (*WA*, VIII, 573), and the
tractate *Eine Predigt, dass Kinder zur Schule halten solle* (*WA*, XXX, 2,
576). The latter passage is a brief but ringing tribute to the parent, written
soon after his death.

into the convent.[5] These statements date from various periods in his life and are of importance as indexing a childhood peculiarly sensitive to fears. The superstitions which begirt his childhood and which were to play so large a part in his later thinking were a part of the equipment of both lay and clerical circles, as may be seen by paralleling the catalogs of harmful spirits furnished by Luther with those contained in the lists in the *Malleus Maleficarum* or collections of narratives like those by Cæsar of Heisterbach.

Similarly, his school life was, so far as the sources go, bare of unusual features. Nothing points to the fact that Luther's arraignment of school methods, particularly school discipline, in the educational tractate *To the Councillors of All German Cities*,[6] was peculiarly applicable to the schools which he attended. His year in Magdeburg was marked by safeguards which secured the adolescent boy such protection as the later Middle Ages could furnish. An older boy, Johann Reinecke, the son of a neighbor and later a warm friend through life, accompanied him on the journey; and a well-to-do citizen, Paul Mosshauer, formerly of his native city, entertained him with the

---

[5] *"Mei parentes me strictissime usque ad pusillanimitatem coercuerunt. Mein mutter steupet mich vmb einer eingen nuss willen usque ad effusionem sanguinis. Et ita strictissima disciplina me tandem ad monasterium adegerunt, wiewol sie es hertzlich gut gemeint haben, sed ego pusillanimus tantum"* (TR, III, 3566A-1537; cf. TR, II, 2304).

[6] *WA*, XV, 33 (1524).

hospitality of his table.[7] The order of the Brethren
of the Common Life, trained in the moral and religious care of schoolboys, took him under its protection. The fact that contemporary biographers, like
Mathesius, as does Luther himself, mention his begging bread [8] does not lift his school-day habits out of
the normal customs of the time.

The religious impressions formed by the active
participation of the schoolboy in the services of the
choir must have been greatly strengthened by the
surroundings of the Magdeburg year, which came at
the period of adolescence when the pictures which the
boyish mind absorbs are touched with a more intense
coloring. These surroundings were continued during
the three years in Eisenach, where the transition of
the young scholar from boyhood to young manhood
was marked in his memory and that of his contemporaries with the mystic colors of friendship and
romance. These years were accompanied also by the
same protective associations as marked his first journey away from home. It is impossible to interpret
otherwise the facts as set forth by early biographers
and by Luther himself, as well as those which may be
reconstructed out of the contributory data of the
time. Ratzeberger, Luther's family physician, asserts that Martin went to Eisenach, "sent by his

[7] Letter to Claus Sturm, June 15, 1522 (*EA*, LIII, 137).

[8] *Eine Predigt dass man Kinder zur Schule halten solle* (*WA*, XXX, 2, 576 [1530]).

parents to friends," [9] and this is confirmed by another contemporary historian, Mathesius, and by Luther himself, who stated in 1520 that almost all of his relatives were in Eisenach.[10] The husband of his great-aunt, Konrad Hutten, was sacristan of the church of St. Nicholas, and must have shown the boy great kindness, because Luther refers to him in later years with affection, sending him an invitation to his first mass.[11] In spite of his relatives, he recalls in later years that he was a "crumb seeker" and received bread from charity, "especially in my beloved city Eisenach." [12] Again, when in his *Frau Musica* (1538) he speaks of the wretched condition of the singing scholars, he is doubtless citing memories of Eisenach days. Such hardships were inseparable from medieval school life and cannot have lasted long, for in the *Table Talk* he states that after begging his bread from door to door he finally came to "Henricianus" and conducted his son to school, undoubtedly a reference to Heinrich Schalbe, who belonged to a well-known family and was Consul in Eisenach 1495-99.[18]

[9] Cf. C. G. Neudecker, *Die handschriftliche Geschichte Ratzebergers über Luther und seine Zeit*, Jena, 1850, 43.

[10] Letter to Spalatin, Jan. 14 (*Enders*, II, 293).

[11] *Enders*, I, 2; O. Clemen, *Beiträge zur Reformationsgeschichte*, I, 1902, S. 1ff.

[12] *WA*, XXX, 2, 576.

[13] *TR*, V, 5362-1540. Luther's gratitude to the Schalbe family is evidenced by efforts which he made thirty years later to protect a member of it, Caspar Schalbe, possibly a son of his Eisenach patron. Cf. *Enders*, V, 366; *EA*, LIII, 398; LIV, 50.

Out of material furnished by two contemporary biographers a story has been constructed involving a Frau Cotta, which is not justified by the sources, but which when stripped of its romantic features furnishes further evidence of the protective influences which surrounded the youth's study in Eisenach. Ratzeberger tells us that Luther lodged with "Cuntz Kotten," [14] while Mathesius refers to a "devout matron" who took the boy into her house and to her table, "because on account of his singing and earnest prayer in the churches she conceived an affection for him." Taken together, the sources indicate that at least in the later years of his Eisenach stay he found hospitality with two distinguished families of the city, the Schalbes and the Cottas, families which were not only of wealthy patrician stock, but also noted for their piety.

The association with religious establishments and clerical persons which the sources indicate for Magdeburg become unmistakable for Eisenach and carry through into the cloister life. Contemporary documents emphasize the wealth of religious foundations in the city. Three great parish churches, one of them of collegiate dignity, had extensive holdings and privileges. Cistercians, Dominicans, Franciscans and Carthusians had cloisters within the walls of the little city. It has been estimated that during Luther's school years no less than three hundred clerical persons found

[14] *Op. cit.*, 43.

a living in this "genuine religious warehouse and nest of priests," as Luther calls it.[15]   At the foot of the Wartburg, overhanging the town, stood a little cloister of Franciscan monks, known as the "Schalbe Collegium" because of the generous support by this family.   Luther later refers to his friend Heinrich Schalbe as the "prisoner and servant" of the Barefoot Monks. It was probably through him that the boy came into close relations with this group of religious, so that ten years later he praises the men of the Collegium and invites them to his first mass.[16]   Another friendship which persists into the convent years is that for Johann Braun, one of the vicars of the Frauenkirche, whom Luther also ardently invites to his first mass.[17]

Along with these personal religious influences came that of the Latin school, then under the rectorate of Johann Trebonius, who appears in the early Luther biographies as a thorough and clever teacher and a humane and liberal man.   The record of Luther at the university and the feeling of gratitude with which he looks back on the Eisenach circle of friends, teachers and associates testify to the fine character of the school.[18]   There is, to be sure, no evidence that the

[15] Cf. W. Rein in *Zeitschrift des Vereins für thüringische Geschichte*, V, 1863, 11.

[16] *Enders*, I, 3ff.; cf. Köstlin-Kawerau, *Luthers Leben und Schriften*, 5. Aufl., 1903, I, 28.

[17] In another letter of the same time he refers to him as *"mei amantissimum."* (Quoted by Scheel, *Luther*, I, 8, 109, Anm. 17.)

[18] Cf. letter regarding Wigand Güldenapf, Aug. 30, 1516; also letter of May 14, 1526 (*EA*, LIII, 378).

humanistic enthusiasms which had already found their way across the Alps into the better schools of southwestern Germany and the lower Rhine country, like those of the Brethren of the Common Life at Schlettstadt or Zwolle, had as yet affected the Eisenach school, where the instruction was probably still the traditional course of the "Trivial" school. The older biographers tell us that Luther was introduced to the "*artes dicendi et poesin*," [19] which probably means the medieval rhetoric as set forth in the mnemonic hexameters of Alexander de Ville Dieu.[20] Melanchthon states further that Luther learned Latin grammar "to the end," [21] which is confirmed by his fluent command of the vernacular of scholars a few years later in the Erfurt cloister. Indeed, the testimony of his later capacity argues against any bitter conflict with poverty at this period and supports the statement of biased witnesses like Melanchthon, Ratzeberger and other contemporary biographers, that he threw himself into his tasks with untiring energy. The texture of his early training as a linguist is shown by his mastery of Greek and Hebrew at Wittenberg in the midst of the bitterest polemical crisis of his life. He was, according to the standards of his time, an ac-

[19] Ratzeberger, *op. cit.*, 44.

[20] The *Doctrinale*, a widely used handbook of the later Middle Ages, which the Humanists did not altogether discard. A list of two hundred and twenty-eight manuscripts and two hundred and seventy-nine editions has been compiled. Cf. Fr. Paulsen, *Geschichte des gelehrten Unterrichts in Deutschland*, I, 48.

[21] "*Hic absolvit grammaticum studium*" (*op. cit.*, VI, 157).

curate philologian, and in Latin he wielded a fluent though rugged style.

This enthusiasm and industry in study Luther must have carried with him to the university. The influence of the Erfurt university upon his choice of the monastic career and its importance for his religious development have been much discussed in the past dozen years, and the researches of Kalkoff [22] and Benary [23] have amended somewhat the picture which had been drawn in the preceding decade by Oergel, [24] Neubauer [25] and others, while the truly encyclopedic analysis of his university studies by Scheel [26] has made possible a clearer understanding of the factors which composed his education. Erfurt was not only the scene of his university training in the scholastic philosophy and such of the natural sciences as went to furnish his mind with the wisdom of the age in this field. It was also at Erfurt that he underwent his early theological training and gave his first lectures on a theological subject. Erfurt saw him inducted into the religious life. Here he took his early vows, celebrated his first mass and fought out the first struggles which a study of Biblical and patristic sources, joined to a sense of disappointment with

[22] Paul Kalkoff, *Humanismus und Reformation in Erfurt*, Halle, 1926.

[23] Fried. Benary, *Zur Geschichte der Stadt u. der Universität Erfurt am Ausgang des Mittelalters*, hrsg. von W. Overmann, 1919.

[24] W. Oergel, *Vom jungen Luther*; Erfurt, 1899.

[25] T. T. Neubauer, *Luthers Frühzeit*, Erfurt, 1917.

[26] *Martin Luther*, I, Kap. 4.

cloister life, brought upon him. For the period of his religious development Erfurt is as important as Wittenberg.

The choice of the university of Erfurt was so natural for Luther as to need scarcely a word of comment. It was the only institution for general study in Germany between Cologne and Leipsic. The city was impressive through its size and trade, being regarded as the most populous city in the Empire.[27] The fertility of its environs and the wealth of its citizens made an impression on the student Luther which he registers after the lapse of many years in his *Table Talk*.[28] Erfurt was, however, at that time approaching a crisis which was rooted in political causes and foreboded economic disaster. The municipal council had been engaged for many years in a bitter struggle to preserve the independence of the city from the encroachment of the Archbishopric of Mainz, which exercised rights of capital judgment over the citizens and sought with the aid of powerful religious organizations within the walls to extend its authority over the council. The latter found backing with the Elector of Saxony, and the city was able to maintain its independence between Archbishop and Elector only through great financial sacrifices. When

[27] The population statistics of German cities at the end of the fifteenth century are quite unreliable. Cf. T. T. Neumann, *Mitteilungen d. Vereins für Geschichte von Erfurt*, XXIV, 1913, p. 13. He puts the population of the city in 1493 at 16,981 (p. 26).

[28] *TR*, III, 2871, a and b-1533; III, 3517; cf. II, 2494.

Luther came to Erfurt these had already begun to bring distress upon the citizens, who under the appearance of prosperity were also struggling with the results of conflagrations, pestilence and floods. Benary-Overmann's work shows how the diplomacy of Mainz added fuel to the flame, until in 1509, the year in which Luther delivered his first lectures in the Augustine convent, revolution broke out, accompanied by a complete economic collapse, and introduced a period of semi-anarchy that did not subside until many years after Martin's departure from the city.

All these disorders play no part in Luther's early correspondence and call forth scarcely any reflection in his later memories. Not even a terrible "town and gown" riot of 1510, the last of many conflicts, which ended in the burning of the university's largest college, the Collegium Majus, with its valuable library, is mentioned, although the Augustine monastery stood near the scene of destruction. Nevertheless, the disorders may have caused the hostile attitude which Luther later shows toward the citizenry of Erfurt. "A bawdy house and a beer house," [29] he calls it many years afterwards. His criticisms of the morals of the citizens smack somewhat of the sort of recollection which an alumnus is apt to retain of his Alma Mater and do not justify the conclusion that Luther himself encountered serious moral dangers in

[29] *TR*, II, 2719b; cf. II, 2800a-1532.

his university years. There is no evidence of this in the sources.

After the middle of the fifteenth century Erfurt had a larger registration than any other university on German soil,[30] although at the time of Luther's entrance the intellectual life of the institution had reached a certain stagnation which was not broken until the reformatory and humanistic movement of two decades later.[31] In any event, the young student entered an institution of great prestige and wealth, with all the guarantees of a sharp personal and individual control of student life that belonged to the discipline of the late medieval German university.

Owing to the generous support of his father, Martin was able to pay his whole fee of twenty groschen in advance *("totum")* and was inscribed on the records as "possessing funds" *("in habendo")*. It could not be without influence on the bearing of the youth in later life that for the four crucial years of university studies he was not obliged to walk in the narrow ways of a poor student. Nor can one refrain from reflection on the contrasts in character of the two men when we recall that just in these years Erasmus, who had been obliged to learn all the devious ways of those who sit as poor guests at the tables of the rich, had returned from his happy visit to Eng-

[30] H. Denifle, *Die Universitäten des Mittelalters*, I, 412.
[31] Kalkoff, *op. cit.*, 2ff.

land to his "Gallic dung-heap" to continue a life of wandering and begging.

The protective care which Luther had enjoyed in his school years was replaced by a strict academic control at the university. The college or Bursa of St. George in which he lived,[32] like the other colleges grouped about the university, formed a state within an academic republic and regulated every step in the life of the student. A master of arts watched over the course of each younger student. The rector and dean of the university visited the Bursa quarterly and inquired into the character of individual students.[33] All through the statutes of the university, as well as those of one of the colleges, the Porta Coeli, which cannot have been very different from those of Luther's college, St. George, there appears an earnest effort on the part of the university to check luxury and immorality. No student was admitted to the final examination unless the supervising master of arts would testify to his solidity of character, and this had to be confirmed by a special examining commission. An underlying effort is apparent in the statutes to approximate life in the Bursa to the monastic model. Thus the inmates of the Porta Coeli were required to pray through the whole Psalter once every

[32] O. Clemen, *Beiträge zur Reformationsgeschichte*, I, 1902, 3f.

[33] "*Älteste noch vorhandene Statuten der Universität vom Jahre 1447*," published in the "*Acten der Erfurter Universität*," I (*Geschichtsquellen der Provinz Sachsen*, Bd. VIII, 1). Cf. especially, Rubrica III, Section 20 (p. 11), and Rubrica IX, Section 15 (p. 22), and *passim*.

fifteen days, with other prayers; and at table the Bible was read and interpreted.[34]

Undoubtedly, even under such control many students were to be found who indulged in dissipation. Charges of this kind which have been occasionally brought against young Luther find no support in the sources. Later on when Luther charged brutally one of his bitterest opponents, Heinrich Emser, a former Erfurt student, with having lost his virtue, the latter admitted the truth of the assertion and replied that he could also charge Luther with "shameful things" ("*flagitia*"). He did not specify these and it is a fair assumption [35] that, in view of Emser's provocation, his character and the blunt speech of the time, he would certainly have certified to a list of immoralities if he had known them.

Indeed, an enumeration of the studies required of the students and an inspection of Luther's academic record at Erfurt, construed in the light of the standards of the time, offer strong evidence of industry and sobriety. We owe to Scheel a systematic statement of the work which was required of a candidate for the bachelor's and master's degree, based on a study of the statutes of the university and other

[34] As further evidence of the monastic character of student life may be cited a requirement of the Collegium Majus that a student holding a stipend thank God once a week for having been born a man and not a woman! (Quoted by Scheel, from the Statutes in the Erfurt Stadtbibliothek.)

[35] Henri Strohl, *L'évolution réligieuse de Luther*, Strasbourg, 1922, 54; cf. Grisar, *Luther*, 1911, I, 20.

contemporary sources.[36] The graduation requirements represent an iron-clad system of academic control as strict as that which supervised the student's personal comings and goings. For the baccalaureate degree one and one-half years were required as a minimum, and Luther applied for his degree in the shortest possible time. The Trivial schools at Mansfeld, Magdeburg and Eisenach had all an exclusively linguistic training; nevertheless such authors as Boethius, Plautus and Terence formed the basis for advanced instruction in these pre-humanistic schools, and these as well as the ingenious hexameters of the medieval rhetoric, the *Doctrinale* of Alexander, which the scholars must memorize, furnished material for lessons in ethics which Luther's teachers can hardly have overlooked. No sharp line of division was drawn between the subject matter of instruction in school and university. Luther's studies at Erfurt must have begun with a review of Latin grammar and further practice in literary forms, based on the *Doctrinale*. These were probably followed by lectures on rhetoric from Petrus Hispanus and an introduction to logic through the *Analytics* of Aristotle. Logic formed the subject of study in the second and third semesters of the candidate for the bachelor's degree, Aristotle and his medieval interpreter Por-

[36] Scheel, *op. cit.*, I, Kap. 4, Par. 13; cf. *"Acten der Erfurter Universität"* (*loc. cit.*, II, 143ff.): *"Statuta examinandos pro baccalauriatu concernencia,"* where the graduation oath of the bachelor is given, as well as other statutes setting forth the material included in the course.

phyrius *(Isagoge)* furnishing the material for the lectures. These taught the young student the laws of demonstration and proof and together with Aristotle's *Refutation of the Sophists* gave him the tools for the disputational exercises which were required of every candidate. The bachelor's preparation was completed by a series of lectures on the *Physics* of Aristotle, including his books *On the Soul,* and a series on spherical astronomy.

These studies were supposed to cover one and one-half years. They introduced the student theoretically to the implements of knowledge—grammar and logic —and to the use of these in presenting thought through logic and rhetoric. They were followed by further training in logic for the master of arts degree. The oath required of the candidates for the master's at Erfurt in Luther's day certified to preparation in mathematics and a month of lectures on music. About one-half of the time seems to have been given to topics in moral philosophy, including Aristotle's *Nicomachean Ethics,* his *Apologetics* and *Household Economy.*

All of this formed only a part of the work of the young candidate. The medieval system, as is well known, presented the student with a highly unified system of knowledge, based in the main on Aristotle as interpreted and arranged by the schoolmen of the thirteenth and fourteenth centuries. The aim of all instruction was by no means a preparation to add to this body of knowledge or correct it, but a training in the efficient and scholarly use of the weapons which it supplied for a further interpretation of the body of knowledge itself. Thus from the first constant practice was required in the disputation. Here the student learned to fence and parry, always in Latin, within the rules prescribed by masters like Lombard and Aristotle. The disputation introduced him to the laws of pure thought without relation to content and trained him in finding the road to final proof through the syllogism. Luther was obliged from the beginning of his course to take part in these exercises and they formed a part of the day's work in the Bursa and in the hall of the faculty of the university until his master's examination.

That he was an able and industrious student is attested by the university records, supported by the testimony of at least one contemporary scholar. Johann Jäger, better known by his humanistic name of Crotus Rubeanus, was one of a small but eminent group of scholars who a decade later formed the advanced guard of the New Learning in central Germany. He was three years older than Luther and during the latter's years of study was engaged in teaching at the university. He knew the young Mansfeld student well, and declared in a letter in 1520 that Martin passed as an "erudite philosopher" among his fellows.[37] The records show that Luther received both his bachelor's and master's degree within the briefest time permitted by the statutes, in itself testimony to industry and moral stability.

Evidence is offered by the sources that there were at least two among his professors who exercised significant influence on his character. The older of these, Jodocus Trutvetter of Eisenach, a highly formalistic schoolman, gained Luther's respect by his deep learning—"the prince of dialecticians of our age," [38] Luther calls him a dozen years later—and apparently his affections as well. In the troubled years following the outbreak of the struggle over indulgences Luther sought a conference with him and was deeply grieved at the profound difference of opinion which had now developed between them.[39] The other, Bartholomew Arnold of Usingen, he praises later as "the best theologian and scientific guide" for younger men, especially as a guide in religious matters.[40] The references to Usingen indicate that in his years as a student of scholastic philosophy Luther found comfort in his religious doubts with this sympathetic teacher. After he had himself be-

---

[37] . . . "eras in nostro quontuberinio musicus et philosophus eruditus" (Ulrich von Hutten, Opera, ed. Böcking, I, 1859, 340). Cf. also the testimony of a bitter enemy, Johannes Cochlaeus, Commentaria de actis et scriptis Martini Lutheri, 1549, p. 1.

[38] Letter to Spalatin, Feb. 22, 1518 (Enders, I, 160).

[39] Letter to Trutvetter, May 9, 1518 (Enders, I, 187).

[40] . . . "optimum paraclitum et consolatorem" (letter to Leiffer, April 15, 1516; Enders, I, 31).

come professor of theology, his former teacher followed him into the Augustine monastery (1512).

The influence of the four years at the Erfurt university was indeed of great importance for the development of Luther's religious character. Later on more than one occasion, he speaks contemptuously of university learning and the Humanist Melanchthon declares that the dialectical tyranny at Erfurt had restrained his moral and religious development. His studies there, however, set their stamp ineradicably upon the means which he employed for the presentation of thought, as well as on the contents of his philosophical thinking. The mechanical technique of his logical training appears more or less in all of the works between 1517 and 1521. The *Ninety-five Theses* against indulgences, the Heidelberg disputation of 1518, the *Resolutions* which are his formal defense of his position in the summer of that year, are all cast in the forms in which he had been trained in the refectory of St. George's Bursa and the hall of the Erfurt faculty. Especially is this true of the three great reformatory tractates of 1520. The whole framework of the address *To the German Nobility*, with its attack on the papal citadel guarded by its threefold ring-wall, shows the result of the author's severe training in logical presentation. This training also evidences itself in the basic structure which supports the fiery eloquence of *On the Freedom of a Christian*, while the dialectical subtleties of the *Baby-*

lonian Captivity of the Church lead back not only to
the preparation afforded by the tractates of Peter
Lombard and the *Categories* and *Topics* of Aristotle,
but also by the latter's *Refutation of the Sophists*
(*De sophisticis elenchis*). For the birth of the Reformation as well as for Luther's own religious
thought, it was of importance that he was trained at
a university which was especially strong on the side
of dialectics, and he carried through life a profound
respect for this method of determining truth, as well
as for the training which dialectics gives in presenting that which one already knows.[41] So persuaded
was he of the value to him of his experience in the
technique of the disputation in several important
crises of his life that he exerted himself to bring these
exercises back into use at Wittenberg in 1532.

Of equal importance for the development of his
religious thought was the character of his studies at
Erfurt in the philosophy of Aristotle, with its
medieval and post-medieval adjustments. The struggle regarding the *universalia,* involving two theories
of the epistemological bases of human thought, had
long since passed through its acute stage in the
German universities when Luther became a student at
Erfurt. Both the *via antiqua* and the *via moderna,*
as the systems of Anselm and of William of Occam
were called, were represented side by side at most
universities of the Empire, and recent researches of

[41] *TR,* II, 2629-1532.

the late Friedrich Benary show that even at Erfurt, formerly regarded as a citadel of the "modernists," the two schools lived peaceably together.[42] But the university teachers who were of importance for Luther, Trutvetter and Usingen, were hard and fast modernists—the former indeed of a stagnated sort— and their great pupil received the stamp of Nominalism from them. Proudly he ranges himself in the storm and stress of 1520 on the side of the "moderns," proudly he puts on the badge of Occam: [43] *"Sum enim Occanicae factionis"*—"For I am of Occam's party!" he declares in his reply to the papal bull of excommunication.[44]

It is hardly necessary to say that the entire dispute between Realists and Nominalists which racked the world of later medieval thought was something more than a debate over a problem in cognition. Siebeck [45] has drawn a contrast between Occam's practical English nature and the refined intellectualism of late classical origin of his Continental predecessors, with its demand for a strictly dialectical and critical foundation of faith. He finds in Occam an influence of the Franciscan tendency which regarded theology less as a subject for dogmatic systematizing than as

[42] *Via Moderna und Via Antiqua*, 57.

[43] . . . *"scilicet Occanicae seu modernorum, quam penitus inhibitam teneo"* (*WA*, VI, 195).

[44] *WA*, VI, 600. That this statement was made in bitter jest does not impair its truth.

[45] *"Occams Erkenntnislehre," Archiv f. Philosophie*, 1897, S. 317ff.

furnishing a basis for an ethical view of life. Certain it is that the separation of faith from a merely speculative conception of the world which appears as a methodical practice throughout Nominalist thought, the separation of theology and philosophy, belongs to Luther's most fundamental ideas.

No less important for him was the Occamist attitude toward the will. Here the struggle over the *universalia* was in fact a reaction of the voluntarist principle against the super-intellectual theorizing of the schoolmen. This phase of the scholastic debate is of great significance for Luther's development, a significance which will become apparent when we follow him into his cell at Erfurt and examine his early lectures to his theological students at Wittenberg. In asserting that it was the ideas and not the objects which had reality, the early scholastic theologians accepted a basis for cognition quite in accord with the intellectual cast of their entire system of penitence and grace. The world of phenomena, as they held, mirrors itself in the human consciousness in general and ideal forms, and consequently the whole structure built upon cognition floats in an atmosphere of pallid intellectualism. It was in Aristotle himself that the leader of the attack on the Realists, William of Occam, found his weapons, for the Stagirite had taught that the object of cognition transforms the observer in such a way that an intellectual similarity arises in him to the thing observed, the so-called "reception of form." [46] Here the "Doctor Singularis," as Occam's admirers called him, seized hold and went a step further. The will, he holds, does not merely mirror the object, transforming it from the sensual into the intelligible (*species sensible* into the *species intelligible*), but it *reproduces* it through an activity of its own. Thus knowledge rests not on the entry of the outer world into us, but on an experience which we undergo. As there can be no experience of God, so there can be no knowledge of Him. The objective basis of faith falls outside the field of logic and knowledge and belongs to mystic intuition. [47] Reason must stop short of the truths of faith and is ineffectual as a plummet for sounding the supernatural world. Faith and knowledge become non-tangent spheres. Theology separates from philosophy and ceases to be a science. The doctrines of faith are not demonstrable. Their field is that of a supernatural reality.

This was the theory which Luther received at Erfurt and which remained the logical basis of his thought throughout life. As set forth by a theologian like Trutvetter and an earnest, godly man like Usingen (in his *Parvulus philosophiae naturalis,* 1499), it appealed alike to the reason and the imagination. Far above philosophy, which can throw only the light of reason on nature, thrones inspired knowl-

[46] Siebeck, *op. cit.,* 321ff.   [47] *Ibid.,* 327.

edge, which is guaranteed by the authority of the Church derived from the Holy Ghost. The truths of theology may be false in philosophy, but they are true nevertheless and whatever contradicts them is wrong. There is then no double truth and no double morality. The canon of the Holy Catholic Church, with its dicta regarding the fates and fortunes of the soul, its doctrines respecting Divine Providence and the miracles, is true as a matter of course. In the world of the spiritual, God's will works supreme and incomprehensible. With arbitrary selection and for reasons not intelligible to us He has chosen a way of salvation and it remains the only way.

"Modernist" in the technical sense only, Luther's teachers, so far as we can identify them, were all men of the older scholastic sort. Erfurt's fame as the greatest of German universities, so that Luther dubs all others mere "Freshmen Schools" in comparison, was founded on a sound and thorough presentation of scholastic philosophy, and does not seem to have been affected appreciably up to this time by the humanistic reforms which within less than two decades after Luther's matriculation, under the leadership of Justus Jonas, were to work such striking changes in the content and method of the university's instruction. Some of these changes were indeed already projecting their influence into German university life: the development of the study of Roman law had already brought increased dignity and importance to university education and increased demand for men of training and culture, influences which Erfurt felt in common with other higher institutions of Germany. The crowded condition of the schools and universities and the restlessness of the schoolboys swarming along the roads toward the larger cities gave evidence that a new spirit was abroad. Erasmus had already begun to direct his attempts at reform squarely at university men, and his efforts to found a new and humanistic school of theology in place of the old scholastic one cannot have passed unnoticed at Erfurt.

Indeed humanistic scholarship had made its entry there into the field of philology. Nicholas Marschalk began in the year 1501 his first interpretations of Greek authors in Erfurt, but soon withdrew from the university. In the neighboring city of Gotha, Konradt Mudt (Mutianus Rufus) had settled after his return from association with humanistic circles in Italy. The learned friend of Pico della Mirandola had brought back with him many ideas of Neo-Platonism and gradually drew around him a group of younger men who made sport of mass, fasts and confession—and it must be said of common morality and decency also—and fired many shafts of wit at the old theologians.[48]

[48] Strauss, *op. cit.*, 34ff.

It is very unlikely that Luther knew Mutianus at this period. Kalkoff's recent putting together of the evidence demonstrates to the point of practical certainty that it was not until 1515, and through Johann Lang, Luther's most intimate cloister friend, that Martin became acquainted with the satirical canon of Gotha.[49] The only outspoken humanist whom Luther knew well was the sharp-tongued Johann Jäger, who as Crotus Rubeanus wrote ten years after Luther entered the monastery the first half of the *Letters of Obscure Men*. During Luther's student days, however, Crotus seems to have cultivated mainly university interests. He took his degree the year of Martin's matriculation, but seems to have belonged, as we have seen, to the same *consortium* with him in Luther's later student days, although there is no proof whatever of any community of interest at this time. Erfurt was at that time and remained for years afterwards a citadel of Scholasticism, in spite of some stimulation of interest in classical authors at the university and the appearance from the Erfurt press of the first Greek lexicon published in Germany, as well as the first Greek grammar and Greek anthology.[50] As late as 1514, Mutianus asserts in his gentle fashion

[49] Cf. correspondence of Mutianus and Lang in 1515 (*Geschichtsquellen d. Provinz Sachsen*, XVIII, 490); cf. also Scheel, *op. cit.*, I, 223.

[50] By Nikolaus Marschalk in 1501 (Paulsen, *op. cit.*, I, 72ff.). Cf. also P. Kalkoff, *Humanism und Reformation in Erfurt, 1500-1530*, 1926, who shows that the transfer of Erfurt to the side of Humanism did not take place until 1519-20, under the leadership of Justus Jonas.

that the "apes of theology and the sophists" dominated the whole school.[51]

Such classical material as Luther absorbed belonged to the furniture of the medieval classroom, and it is extremely unlikely that such interpretations as he heard at the university contained the Neo-Platonic ideas with which the Italian Humanists and their German pupils were occupied. Brought up on Donatus, Priscian, Cato [52] and Alexander de Ville Dieu, he read, according to his own statement,[53] as his first poet, Baptista Mantuanus, whose eclogues against love and in praise of the monastic life had just appeared in Germany. His further intensive reading included Ovid's *Heroïdes* and Virgil, Cicero and Livy, and he had a speaking acquaintance with Juvenal, Horace, Plautus and Terence. Of Greek he knew as yet nothing and was obliged to learn it afterwards in the monastery. His knowledge of classical antiquity was still confined to the orthodox scholastic texts.

After the baccalaureate year, devoted to the use of the implements of knowledge—grammar, rhetoric

[51] Cf. *Geschichtsquellen der Provinz Sachsen*, 1890, Nos. 418, 419. Luther's friendship with Humanists like Peter Eberbach, George Spalatin and Johann Lang belongs to the years after he entered the cloister. These men were pupils of Marschalk, but there is nothing in the sources to show that Luther was. Before he had gone far in his theological studies the influence of the Humanists became of importance in giving him an attitude of respect for a thorough and exact study of the sources.

[52] Cf. his praise of Cato, Aesop and Donatus (*TR*, III, 3490-1536).

[53] *TR*, I, 256-1532.

and logic—came the year of preparation for the master's degree, which introduced him to the elements of the medieval system of knowledge of natural and moral philosophy. Their substantive bases were furnished by Aristotle, whose system, with its scholastic interpretations and their fourteenth-century modifications, formed the framework within which Luther's teachers set forth their ideas of nature and the mind of man. Thus Aristotle formed the basis for his ideas of the universe, and in spite of the changes which later study wrought in his theological conceptions, the Greek philosopher, with his scholastic and post-scholastic interpreters, remained throughout life the foundation for his thinking. That which seems to have impressed him most in later years when reviewing his studies was the sense of formal power which Aristotle gave in the search for truth. The patterns of thought which he received from the Occamist school of theology turned him early in his theological studies against the Greek philosopher as a spiritual guide. As early as the marginal notes of 1509, which formed the basis for his lectures on Lombard's *Sentences* at the Erfurt university or monastery, he criticizes Aristotle sharply for having a false view of eternal life;[54] and in 1518 in the fire of his enthusiasm for reforming the curriculum at Wittenberg on humanistic lines he rages against the Stagirite, branding his ethics as something which suits theology

[54] *WA*, IX, 26, 99.

"like the wolf the lamb." [55] Nevertheless, in the measured presentation of the address *To the Christian Nobility of Germany* he calls for the retention in the educational system of Aristotle's books on logic, rhetoric and poetics,[56] and a dozen years later in his *Table Talk* praises him repeatedly for his "exact method." [57] The body of knowledge of the natural sciences which Luther carried through life was that which he derived from his study of Aristotle's works.[58] In fact, although his knowledge of nature is narrow in scope, it is by no means lacking in accuracy of details, and his views of natural phenomena, wherever free from the superstitious apparatus of childhood, show considerable liberality. To the Greek philosopher he owed his knowledge that the earth is round and small in comparison with the stars,[59] while his theory of the movement of the earth is exactly in Aristotle's manner,[60] and he clung through life to Aristotle's statement regarding the nature of creatures.

[55] Letter to Spalatin, Sept. 2, 1518 (*Enders*, I, 227).
[56] *WA*, VI, 458.
[57] *TR*, II, 2412-1532; III, 3608d-1537.
[58] *TR*, II, 2159-1531.
[59] *TR*, II, 2413b-1532.
[60] *TR*, II, 2730a-1532.

III

THE ENTRY INTO THE MONASTERY

We have now traced in some detail the facts with respect to the education of Luther, so far as they are available in the sources at our command. These sources, covering the school and university years, except for those taken from the university records, are drawn for the most part from Luther's sermons and *Table Talk* and date at least a quarter of a century after the completion of his academic studies. But the tireless investigation of older and younger scholars who have devoted their labors to the Erfurt university at this period—Köstlin, Oergel, Neubauer, Scheel, Kalkoff and Benary, to mention only the most prominent—enables us to check in considerable measure Luther's statements and those of his earlier biographers, his friends and associates, Melanchthon, Mathesius and Ratzeberger, who may be supposed to have discussed the details of Luther's life with their older and revered master. The resulting picture of the young man's preparation down to the beginning of the cloister years, controlled by the general studies of the scholastic universities by Denifle and Paulsen, is a fairly complete one and it may be doubted whether any new sources which may be discovered will throw further light upon it. It shows a young North German of middle-class birth as well protected from moral and physical dangers as the conditions of the time permitted, and furnished with adequate material support, enjoying such opportunities for a scientific education as the schools and universities of the late scholastic period offered. Thus far his course may be regarded as lacking in unusual features in comparison with that of other gifted youths of his time preparing for a learned career. The philosophical basis upon which his religious thought was to be founded had been provided him in the study of the Nominalists. His knowledge of the literature and history of the past was apparently limited to the traditional medieval and classic authors. His conception of the physical world must have been a mixture of the superstitions of earlier life and the physical and biological works of Aristotle which, together with the medieval works on astronomy, defined his ideas of the universe.

How far the young student occupied himself with thoughts of God's ways to man, we do not know. It is probable that as yet he accepted the Aristotelian ideas with their Thomistic interpretations and their Occamist modifications passively and blindly. There is no evidence that university studies aroused skeptical ideas on his part. The statement ascribed to him many years later that as a master of arts he became addicted to reading the Bible, and from a mere reading of the text recognized that there were many errors in the papacy, finds no confirmation; [1] on the other hand, when as an old man he sketched his theological development down to 1517, he refers to the whole university period as one of blind obedience to the Pope. Occamist ideas of the soul dominated his thought in all the years to come, and he carried with him through life something of the militancy of his Erfurt teachers against the hair-splitting of the Thomists. It is this that armed his bitter attacks on "philosophy" in his mature years, when he had come to regard the Aristotelian scholastic studies as a false substitute for a knowledge of the Bible. In 1521 he arraigns the Thomistic philosophy bitterly for its heretical teaching and urges young men to avoid it as they would the destruction of their own soul. [2] Already five years earlier in his lectures on Romans he had charged his students to learn to know Christ and Him crucified and to treat philosophy as a subject that one must be acquainted with in order to refute it. [3] In 1518 he wrote to his former teacher Trutvetter that he daily prayed to God that in place of the brothers'

[2] *TR*, III, 3593-1537.

[2] *WA*, VIII, 127: *Rationis Latomianae confutatio.*

[3] Denifle, *op. cit.*, I, 2 609ff., shows that while these attacks on philosophy had their roots in Occam's school, nevertheless Luther, beginning with his earliest lectures, develops a bitterness against philosophy and Aristotle in particular quite peculiar to himself.

studies in philosophy some study of the Bible and the Fathers might be introduced.[4]

Thus far the conditions which surrounded Luther's preparation for active life involve no polemical consideration. We now approach a crisis in his life which has long been a subject of bitter discussion—his entry into the monastery and the cloister years at Erfurt. Here the sources are by no means meager, but their value is impaired by their subjective and partisan character. For the six or seven years intervening between Luther's entry into the monastery and his final transfer into the Wittenberg cloister and university we have half a dozen letters from Luther himself, all of them, with one exception, addressed to members of the Erfurt Augustinians. They are of slight significance for a knowledge of his religious development. Further, we have a large mass of material in the *Table Talk,* drawn from Luther's recollections. The first of these notes dates more than twenty years after the event; in general they are made up of random, disconnected remarks reported by pens varying widely in trustworthiness and they have survived at least two centuries of apologistic tradition. Furthermore, we have statements from the early biographers, particularly Melanchthon, regarding Luther's entry into the convent and early monastic experiences, which were, to be sure, furnished by Luther himself, but furnished after a lifetime filled with fierce struggles

[4] Letter of May 15, 1518 (*Enders,* I, 188).

against the old Church.[5] Beyond this there are a few, not more than three or four, notes of recollections on the part of contemporaries who had known Luther in these years, which are pertinent to his religious development. All are touched by the bitterness of the struggle which divided Germans in the first quarter of the sixteenth century. Finally there are passages in the works of Luther, beginning with the lectures on Psalms, that contain material from which inferences may be drawn relating to the growth of his religious ideas in the preceding years. Of these the work *On the Monk's Vow* (1521) is of especial importance.

These sources have of course been canvassed many times. Few have taken the position of Denifle, who regards any conclusion as to this entire period based on Luther's own statements as quite valueless and rejects altogether the *Table Talk* as a basis for the study of his early monastic life. Succeeding Catholic students, like Grisar and F. X. Kiefl,[6] take Luther's religious development very seriously, while almost all of the Protestant investigators, especially since the publication of Denifle's *Luther and Lutheranism,* have turned their attention to the early monastic years. The facts regarding his entry into the convent and the sources of his early theological ideas and his

[5] Melanchthon states in the introduction to Luther's Latin works that Luther had often spoken to him of his entry into the cloister and his life there.

[6] Cf. his important article in *Hochland,* XV, 7, 1.

doubts and soul crises have engaged some of the ablest minds in German Protestantism. It cannot be our duty here to review the conclusions of these scholars or to mark the ebb and flow of Luther research about these points in recent years. Those who are interested may find the problems and the attempts at their solution ably set forth and analyzed by Boehmer, in German,[7] or more recently by Henri Strohl, in French,[8] and in a little book published in America by J. M. Reu.[9] The existence of so large a body of literature on the subject is in itself proof that it is impossible to answer categorically the questions which arise regarding this stage of Luther's religious development. Were the sources much richer than they are, we should obviously be unable to say which of the many motives that contributed to Luther's entrance into monastic life was the deciding one. Nor could we, even if supplied with contemporary material by Luther himself, trace step by step the struggle between doubt and assurance, fear and contentment, nor the birth and growth of ideas respecting divine justice which agitated Luther's soul during this period. Luther's later remarks on the subject, often confusing and sometimes self-contradictory, show that the chief actor himself was, in later years, far from clear regarding the chronology of his progress

[7] *Luther im Lichte der neueren Forschung*, Leipzig, 1906. The later editions have undergone sharp revision.

[8] *L'évolution religieuse de Luther*, Strasbourg, 1922.

[9] *Luther, 1517-1917*, Chicago, 1917.

in religious thought. The best we can do with the
evidence at hand is to construct an outline of the
development of his early religious thought which
shall be as objective as possible in its interpretation
of the sources, conceding at the same time that such
an outline is after all but an ideology defined by the
limitations of him who draws it up.

As he approached the master's degree, the young
student in the faculty of philosophy had, if we are
right in construing the records of the university,
shown increasing ability and diligence. With the end
of his eighth semester he had attained the degree which
was the preliminary goal of higher studies and entitled
him to membership in the faculty. His father, as
Luther tells us sixteen years later, wanted to bind him
to civil life by an honorable and rich marriage.[10] The
road to civil preferment lay through the study of law,
which then, as now, paved the way to public and
remunerative employment. In May, 1505, we find
him registered in the school of law, it is not certain
whether canon or civil law. A little over two months
later he entered the convent of the Erfurt Augustinians as a novice, to devote himself to the religious life
of the Eremites. What determined this change of
heart and led him to a step involving so momentous a
break with his previous life? Luther himself attempts
to answer this question categorically in the tractate
On the Monk's Vow, which he published in the year

[10] De votis monasticis (WA, VIII, 573).

of the Diet of Worms and dedicated to the father whose plans for him had been so rudely interrupted. He states that he had not entered the monastery voluntarily, but was forced to do so by a vow extorted from him in great peril.[11] This statement, with others by which Luther emphasizes the suddenness of his decision for the monastic life, supported by the evidence of a fellow-student, Crotus Rubeanus, has not satisfied past generations of Luther students in Germany and elsewhere. The older tradition of Luther biographers, that his entry into the cloister was a gradual development of an idea growing out of a life spent amid poverty and was prompted by the fear of God's wrath, is still supported by scholars like Harnack and Preuss. Others ascribe the step to the religious influence of Erfurt; others to the growing fear of death and judgment. Still others, among them the more recent Luther scholars, picture Luther as a youth of normal development whose entry into the monastery was a sudden rupture with his entire past (A. V. Müller, Scheel).

It is true that Luther's entry into the monastery was only one step in his religious life and that the events which followed within the next two years in the cloister are of greater importance for our subject than his entrance into the monastic order. Neverthe-

[11] Neque enim libens et cupiens fiebam monachus, multo minus vero ventris gratia, sed terrore et agonis mortis subitae circumvallatus vovi coactum et necessarium votum" (WA, VIII, 574).

less, this was the first of many characteristic dramatic acts in the religious life of the man and, as such, symptomatic for his later development. It is for that reason that it must be given a careful examination.

Such an examination, however, soon reveals facts which tend to deprive the act of the catastrophal nature which Luther gave to it. Indications are not wanting that powerful subconscious forces had long been at work agitating him and pointing the way toward the portals of renunciation. It may have been the fear of such a step that drove his father, watching with glowing heart the career of the son, to seek to bind him to a civil life by marriage. Another indication is Luther's recommendation, in 1516, of his professor of philosophy, Usingen, as a guide of souls,[12] for as Müller has pointed out,[13] the experiences on which this recommendation rests could have occurred only before Luther's entry into the monastery, since after that he would have been obliged to consult a confessor out of his own order. A passage in the *Table Talk*,[14] supported by the early biographer Mathesius, says that as a bachelor of arts he came upon a Latin Bible in the university library; that he had never seen this before in his life and that he read with great interest the story of Hannah and Samuel. This is possibly an error in the sources, since elsewhere

[12] *"optimum . . . paraclitum et consolatorem"* (letter of April 15, 1516; cf. Enders, I, 31).

[13] A. V. Müller, *Luthers Werdegang bis zum Turmerlebnis*, 1920, 15 and 16.

[14] *TR*, V, 5346-1540.

one of the best-accredited scribes of the *Table Talk*
quotes him as saying that he had read this story as a
boy.[15]   It is quite possible that the reference here is to
the school at Magdeburg, for the Brethren of the
Common Life who looked after him there had as an
especial part of their program the copying of the
Bible and its dissemination.   There is some additional
authority for the assumption that Luther came across
the Vulgate Bible at about twenty years of age.[16]   But
this does not mean that he had not seen beforehand
one of the many German versions of the Bible already
in existence, since it has been abundantly shown that
these were widely known among the laity at the end
of the fifteenth century.[17]   Least of all can such an
hypothesis imply that as boy and young man he was
ignorant of the evangelical texts, such as the epistles
and gospels for the church year, which were to be
found in one of the many "evangelist books" in cir-
culation in Germany at the end of the fifteenth
century.   More convincing still is Luther's subsequent
remarkable power of quoting the Scriptures from
memory, which makes it hard to believe that he was
not familiar with considerable parts of them from

[15] Veit Dietrich (*TR*, I, 116-1531).

[16] *TR*, II, 1552.

[17] No less than seventeen German translations of the Bible were in existence
before Luther, and several well-accredited witnesses at the turn of the century, including Jacob Wimpfeling, the great Alsatian Humanist, testify to the
reading of the Bible on the part of the laity.   Cf. Kerker, "*Zur Geschichte
des Predigtwesens in der letzten Hälfte des 15. Jahrhs*" (*Tübinger Quartal-
schrift*, 1861, S. 373).

childhood. The statement in a well-attested passage in the *Table Talk*, above referred to, that the monks gave him a Bible with a red cover and that he soon made himself familiar with it, [18] may well have been true without impairing the validity of the foregoing conclusion.

The influence of clerical surroundings and associations since youth cannot indeed be overlooked. The young man, who had now reached his twenty-second year, had spent his entire life within the shadow of powerful and revered institutions. The choral associations of the schoolboy had been supplemented by personal intercourse with men of the monastic life in both Magdeburg and Eisenach. This was followed by the semi-monastic life at a university in a city which far surpassed Mansfeld, Magdeburg and Eisenach as an ecclesiastical center. Close to the university lay what was probably the finest group of religious buildings in Germany—the Cathedral, the Severinenstift and the great episcopal residence. Around about was almost every type of medieval Christian institution. Benedictines, Cistercians, Scottish monks, Dominicans and Servants of Mary, with nuns of affiliated and independent orders, came and went on the streets. Each order was housed within the walls of its own building and set apart from the rest of the citizens by the operation of the canon law. Each was equipped with many ancient privileges, such

[18] *TR,* I, 116.

as exemption from taxation and from the rigid regulations which bound the handicrafts and merchant
guilds in the medieval city, and several enjoyed a rich
income from widely distributed lands and from
trading privileges. Some, like the Benedictines, had
within their walls a store of relics which attracted
pilgrimages from without. In every spectacular
phase of public life the clergy dominated, and they
organized processions of great splendor, into which
they marshaled the officers and students of the university and the councilors of the city. The student
Luther may himself have taken part in these semi-
religious festivities which fired the imagination of
young and old.

The mind of the young man, stirred by these outer
influences, was also moved from within, for in spite of
the character of suddenness which he gives to the
circumstances which surrounded his conversion to the
religious life, there is certainly evidence enough in
these scattered recollections—some of which, to be
sure, have come down to us in garbled form—of a
deep stirring of religious emotion that preceded, perhaps by years, the final resolution. As has often been
pointed out, he must have been occupied with the
thought of the convent before the experience in the
forest at Stotternheim, otherwise he would have pro-
nounced some other vow. Evidently the "sturdy
fellow," which Luther says he was at that time,[19] had

[19] TR, I, 116.

within him profound thoughts of man's sin and God's
justice. Echoes of this reverberated in his memory
many years afterwards. Melanchthon, with whom
the older man must have discussed in detail the phases
of his religious development, speaks of the sudden
onsets of fear when thinking of God's wrath "which
almost caused him to pass away." [20]   Deep emotions
of guilt must have tormented him in spite of his love
of merry music and society. Thirty years later the
memory remained of the desperate doubts and fears
that assailed him as a master of arts so that he "went
about sadly," doubts that were by no means allayed
by reading the Bible, since this brought sad thoughts
of the errors of the papacy, whose authority must be
stronger than his.[21]   The latter suggestion probably
sprang from three decades of struggle with the institution in Rome, but the fact of the torment during
his Erfurt student days by doubts of salvation remains. Outer events came to emphasize and intensify
these feelings; but he declares that a sense of fear for
his salvation had not been unknown to him from
early childhood.[22]   To every Catholic of the later
Middle Ages in whom the sense of sin was active the
fear of sudden death presented awful possibilities.

[20] " . . . subito tanto terrores concutiebant, ut pene examinaretur" (Corpus
Reformatorum, VI, 157).

[21] "Illico mihi inciderunt einsmodi cogitationes in bibliotheca Erphurdiensi:
Ecce quam magna autoritas est papae et ecclesiae: soltest dw allain khlug
sein? Ey, dw mochtest irren!" (TR, III, 3593-1537).

[22] Letter to Gerhard Wilscamp, Jan. 1, 1528 (Enders, VI, 173).

Luther states more than once late in life that he rushed into the monastery because he was persuaded by such a life to win more gratitude from God and that he took the vows for the sake of his own safety.[23]

We cannot enter more deeply than this into the state of soul from which sprang the conversion of the young student to the monastic life. We must be content to establish the fact that we have to do with a nature that combined a fiery and vigorous temperament with an especial gift for the other-worldly. As early as 1513 in his lectures on the Psalms he declares that in his youth he felt a repugnance to all preaching about the wrath of God. It is probably one of his own earliest childhood impressions that he recalls when he warns his hearers many years later against such pictures as that of Christ as a judge sitting on a rainbow.[24]

Certain events may well have intensified his fears and prepared the way for action. We may omit a discussion of these, as it is hard to distinguish facts from the legends which the early biographers of Luther wove about his conversion. One fact worthy of mention is attested by university records. Two fellow-students belonging to the same group of sixteen candidates for the master's degree which took the examination with him were carried off by sudden death early in the year, one just before his promotion

---

[23] *Enarratio in Genesin* (*WA*, XLIV, 782; cf. *TR*, IV, 4414).
[24] *TR*, VI, 6628.

to the degree and the other within a few days after he had taken his examination.[25] This event may have made a deep impression upon Luther and may be connected with a statement made both by Melanchthon and Mathesius regarding trouble which the death of a friend caused him at this time.[26]

The sudden catastrophe which was to bring the final resolve impressed date and details upon Luther throughout his life. On July 2, the day of the Festival of Mary, he was overtaken by a violent thunderstorm when close to the village of Stotternheim, not far from Erfurt. A bolt of lightning from the clouds struck near him, knocking him down. Sixteen years later in the work *On the Monk's Vow* Luther recalled vividly the mortal fear of a sudden and unprepared death which flashed through his soul at that desperate moment and wrung from him his vow to become a monk. In these years, when the struggle against the papacy possessed his every thought, he referred to this vow as having been wrung from him by terror,[27] and again and again in the *Table Talk* he assures his hearers that the vow was made under duress, and that he afterwards regretted it and carried it out unwillingly.[28] He represents himself as having de-

[25] Oergel, *op. cit.*, 72ff.

[26] *Ibid.*, 33, 34.

[27] *"neque libens . . . sed vovi coactum et necessarium votum"* (*WA*, VIII, 573).

[28] *"Ego per vim factus sum monachus contra voluntatem patris mei, matris, Dei et Diaboli"* (*TR*, IV, 4414-1539). *"Postea poenituit me voti"* (*TR*, IV, 4707-1539). Cf. *TR*, II, 2286-1531.

layed for fourteen days the fulfillment of his vow.
He could not consult his father, knowing in advance
that the older man's decision would be negative, and
perhaps dreading the determined opposition of the
temperamental miner. His friends tried to dissuade
him, but his decision was unshaken.

Much discussion has taken place in the past decade
among German theologians as to the character of
Luther's vow. Two scholars trained in Catholic
usages, Grisar [29] and Müller,[30] the latter a convert to
Protestantism, have testified to the binding nature
of Luther's oath, and the evidence they adduce based
on medieval and Catholic usage seems overwhelming.
Even without accepting the additional moments by
which contemporaries sought to increase the similarity of Luther's conversion to that of the Apostle
Paul, its sudden and unexpected character stands out
as well authenticated among fellow-students, like
Crotus Rubeanus. As has been pointed out, however,
the vow that sprang from a moment's terror was in
fact the release of subconscious impulses which had in
all probability been of a cumulative sort. Luther records that two years previously, at Whitsuntide,
1503, he had twice been in mortal danger from an
accidental sword wound and that he had on both
occasions called upon the Virgin for help.[31] He re-

---

[29] *Luther*, III, 37, 2.
[30] *Luthers Werdegang bis zum Turmerlebnis*, 3ff.; cf. *Theol. Studien und Kritiken*, 1917, 496.
[31] *TR*, I, 119-1531.

cords no vow at that time, however, but simply states that convalescence brought a revival of his youthful spirits and that he learned to play the lute. The experience in the forest of Stotternheim was only a trigger action for which the growing obsession of fear and the longing for peace had laid the charge. The cumulative memories of the self-sacrificing Brothers of the Common Life who had cared for him, of the men of the Schalbe College in Eisenach who had befriended him, the mystic charm of the life that renounces all that it may win all as shown by the worn and racked body of Brother Ludwig of Madgeburg, bowed under his heavy sack, or the Carthusian monks whom he must have seen daily passing through the streets of Erfurt, worn with fasting and prayer,[32]— all swept him toward the peace of the cloister. Why might he not find the contentment that comes with the loss of all? Why might he not win peace by surrendering all to God? In one of his later lectures a scribe quotes him as saying that he entered the monastery because he had "the persuasion that by this form of life he would offer God a great sacrifice." [33] The path from the university to the cloister was a well-beaten one. Why should he not follow other masters of arts who had gone thither and found the peace which he craved?

---

[32] Oergel, op. cit., 43.

[33] "quia persuasum habebam, me eo genere vitae . . . magnum obsequuum Deo praestare" (WA, XLIV, 782).

Martin's resolution to enter a religious order, like every other resolution which gives to man's life a new direction for years to come, must have sprung from many motives, some of them arising from the profound depths of the subconscious and, therefore, clear to him only years after, if at all. Later on, in reviewing this period, his memory and judgment were clouded by the various struggles which filled the fourth and fifth decades of his life and it is highly doubtful if he was able to do justice to the mystical appeal of the religious life which he felt in the plastic university years. A review of the influences which surrounded his earlier life as well as of his attitude of respect and sympathy for the religious men of Eisenach and for his associates in the Augustinian cloister makes it evident that it was not the fear of God's wrath alone that drove him to renounce the world. To the popular mind the monastic life undoubtedly brought many spiritual rights and privileges which had no authority in religious canon. It is possible that no doctor of the Church in the later Middle Ages would have advocated on theological grounds the idea set forth by Luther in his attack on monasticism, that the entrance into the monastic order was a "new baptism," making one as pure again as when he first emerged from the baptismal waters. The statement has been bitterly attacked by Denifle and other Catholic theologians, but such views were widely held, not merely by the more ignorant ranks of the religious. St. Bernard himself recites nine joys which the religious person has as compared with other Christians,[34] and numerous other witnesses of standing may be cited as supporting the view that the monastic vow was of more effect than the first baptism. As it happened, Luther did afterwards bitterly regret his vow and could only remember that a sense of fear of God's judgment drove him to it: to seek by the monastic vow, as he puts it, to do "more than enough" to be free from his sins and to become better than the rest of the Christians.[35]

The researches of Benary have shown that, of the religious orders in Erfurt which could open their doors to Luther, only that of the Augustinians could appeal to him. Indeed, the choice was so fully in accord with the development of his character that it is a further reason for regarding his entrance upon the monastic life as no sudden development but the next organic step in the growth of the young man's character. His natural vigor as well as his associations in Magdeburg and Eisenach must have directed him early to the mendicant orders, who sought by preaching and the care of souls to fulfill the demands of an increasingly social age. Of these, none could compare in dignity and standing in Erfurt with the congregation of the Order of the Eremites of St. Augustine, whose great complex of buildings lay close

[34] K. Benrath, *Luther im Kloster*, 1905, 29, 30.
[35] *WA*, VIII, 595, 28ff.

to Luther's Bursa. Although the order, at this time, did not enjoy the academic influence which marked it among the Erfurt religious groups in the preceding generation, nevertheless it had a position of prestige gained through a tradition of eminent theological teachers and eloquent preachers. As a result of a vigorous reformation half a century before, thirty cloisters had been brought together into a more strict observance of the Rule of St. Augustine. The cloister which Luther entered had shared in this reformation and was one of the "strict observers"; indeed, under the vigorous direction of Johann von Staupitz, the general vicar of the reformed cloisters, who gave to the order in 1504 a new constitution—a model in its rigid prescription of monastic duty—the Erfurt Congregation distinguished itself by its strict adherence to the provisions of the order and its rigor in conforming to the rules for prayer and the ascetic conduct of life.

It was, then, no order stagnated in medieval conservatism nor in a round of mechanical observances that Luther found represented by the Eremites of St. Augustine at Erfurt. How did the young master of arts and *studiosus juris* meet his obligations as a monk and what was the effect of the observances of the conventual life upon him? On both of these subjects we have a great number of statements from Luther after 1530. A few of them are to be found in his letters and works, but for the most part they are contained in sermons, lectures and in the *Table Talk*, transcribed by others and in part of doubtful text.[36] They vary from assertions of his piety and rigid observance as a monk through cold, fasting, watching and prayers, driving his body in this martyrdom to the point of danger to health, to descriptions of the frightful terrors which he suffered at the name of Christ and his despair of attaining eternal happiness. It has been pointed out that as Luther advances in years these expressions regarding his monastic martyrdom and his disillusionment in his search for peace attain a certain crescendo,[37] and it is true that in the preface of a work written when Luther still wore the cowl, though he was about to lay it aside,[38] he admits "numerous sins and acts of impiety" and states that he had lived as a monk "certainly not without sin but without grave reproach (*crimen*)."

By a study of the constitution of 1504 of the Reformed Congregations, we are able to establish with definiteness the demands made on Luther as novice and after he had made his full profession as a monk. He must first commit to memory the Rule of St. Augustine and a considerable number of the fifty-one chapters of the constitution, making up as a whole an extraordinary code for the sound discipline of a young novice in his relation to God, to his order, and to

---

[36] Strohl has collated these, *L'évolution, etc.*, 78ff.
[37] *Op. cit.* I, 79.
[38] *Devotis monasticis* (*WA*, VIII, 574).

his cloister brethren as individuals. Upon two foundations, training in humility and in brotherly love, there was erected a system of precepts which might well lay iron bonds on individual development. Speaking was not permitted in choir, refectory or cell nor in the common room (*dormitorium*) between eight in the evening and six in the morning, all necessary intercourse being carried on by signs.[39] Laughter was absolutely forbidden. The silence of meals was broken by the reading from a sacred work. Private confession must be made at least once a week; public confession of offenses against rules of the order was required in a full meeting of the chapter. Every slip in the liturgical or ascetic routine brought guilt which must be atoned for by an immediate gesture of humiliation and subsequent penance, while in the case of more serious offenses of the will, the atonement might extend to scourging before the assembled convent, or even to exclusion from the order. It has recently been shown [40] that no less an authority than a head of the Augustine Order, Coriolanus, had declared twenty years earlier (1482) in his commentary on the Rule of St. Augustine that the monks engaged themselves to observe it in all of its parts and that the omission of a single part was a sin (*crimen*), the only dispute being as to whether it constituted a venial or mortal sin. Each morning was spent fast-

---

[39] Cap. 17; cf. Oergel, *op. cit.* 78.
[40] A. V. Müller, *Luthers theologische Quellen*, 1912, 46ff.

ing, and on a number of days the fast was broken
only by the evening meal.

The liturgical demands were in themselves severe
enough to make a life of ascetic routine. The heavy
sleep of the youthful novice on his bed of straw was
broken at three o'clock in the morning by the summons to matins, and as the day swung around the
changing hours were marked by seven or eight gath-
erings of the chapter for prayer. This service in the
choir was constant and exacting both in its demands
on the attention and the memory, and every slip in
Psalter or versicle or any part of the complicated
service must be atoned for.

It must not be forgotten that, even with the rules
of the convent and contemporary interpretations of
them before us, it is not possible to draw an accurate
picture of what they meant in the life and blood
of the observant. Although it is well attested that
the Erfurt congregation was strict and rigid, human
conformity in matters of discipline is far less irksome
than appears from printed regulations, and a common
devotion to an ideal together with a spirit of mutual
love and sympathy, which does not seem to have
been absent from the Erfurt cloister, breathes into
the hardest routine a stern contentment and happiness.

An important rôle in Luther's adaptation must be
assigned to the master of novices, who looked daily
and almost hourly into the soul of his young ward.

After years of warfare against the monastic life, Luther termed the master who had trained him "a truly excellent man, undoubtedly under the damned cowl a true Christian." Evidence of the strong affection between the "fine old man" and the impulsive young novice are to be found in Luther's correspondence and conversations down to his old age.[41]

There is evidence enough that, in spite of the bitter things which Luther later says of the monastic life, he adapted himself to the demands of the order with success, and that in speaking of his novitiate as a period when he was "burning with zeal" he describes not only the earlier years but the greater part of his monastic life. Referring to the time of his first mass, he says he regarded the life in the convent as a "divine life, full of charm and calm."[42] When in 1512 he became a district vicar of the order, his letters attest a deep loyalty to the statutes and a rigid insistence on a full observance of the Rule.[43]

That his life in this period was above reproach is fully attested by contemporary evidence. To quote only hostile witnesses, Flacius Illyricus cites in 1549 an old convent associate of Luther as testifying to the blameless character of his life in the cloister.[44] There is similar evidence in 1531 from Dr. Dungersheim of

[41] Letter to the Elector of Saxony, April 9, 1532 (*de Wette*, IV, 427); cf. *Enders*, IX, 253, Anm. 2.

[42] Scheel, *Dokumente zu Luthers Entwickelung*, 1911, 12; cf. 59.

[43] E.g., letter of May 17, 1517, to the Propst of Liskov (*Enders*, I, 99).

[44] Grisar, *op. cit.*, III, 692; cf. Scheel, *Luther*, II, 337.

Leipsic, Luther's Franciscan critic,[45] and from Nathin, the guide of Luther's theological studies at the Erfurt monastery, while Luther's bitter enemy Cochlaeus admits that he was zealous in his studies and spiritual exercises.[46] The legend that he neglected the liturgical exercises and private prayers required of the Augustinian brethren, whose faithful observance Luther himself praises after ten years of monkdom,[47] is a faithfully cultivated one, but unproven for the first decade of Luther's cloister life. We come upon the first evidence of a neglect of the canonical hours, prayers that lay with especial weight upon the conscience of the monk, in the fall of 1516,[48] at the time of the completion of the lectures on Romans, when Luther complains of a lack of time for these personal religious exercises. He then began to allow them to lapse for two or three weeks; then on a Sunday he would shut himself in and say the prayers which were in arrears throughout the entire day without food or drink.[49]

On the other hand, in view of the impulsive temperament of the man we cannot disregard the testimony of contemporaries (hostile contemporaries, to be sure) that he showed early in his cloister career something of the violence of character and intoler-

[45] Scheel, *op. cit.*, II, 337, Anm. 35.

[46] *Commentaria de actis et scriptis M. Lutheri*, 1549, 1.

[47] Letter of March 1, 1517 (*Enders*, I, 87).

[48] Letter to Lang, Oct. 26 (*Enders*, I, 66).

[49] *TR*, I, 405-1533.

ance of opposition which he carried with him through later life. As early as 1524 Cochlaeus [50] charges him with disputatiousness, even in his novitiate year, while this and other contemporaries claimed to have observed that he was "peculiar." [51] Nathin, his instructor in theology in the year following his profession, noticed in him an "obstinate and almost fanatic spirit." [52] More than one hint of a clash between the young monk, struggling to adjust himself to the common life of the brethren stagnated in the iron framework of their environment, has filtered down to us in the form of legends which will not individually bear the test of historical criticism but nevertheless reflect characteristics which are later so well attested in Luther that they make a strong impression of truth. Such is a story told by John Mathesius in one of his sermons [53] and supported by Dr. Ratzeberger, [54] that the brethren made him do the humblest manual work and sent him with a beggar's bag through the streets. The young master of arts must have given himself up with natural enthusiasm to the demands of theological study, and the difficulty of bringing him under the harsh discipline of cloister democracy is attested in the *Table Talk* [55] and too well founded in psychology not to invite acceptance,

[50] *Paracelsis,* fol. C, 2b; quoted by Scheel, *Luther,* II, 336.

[51] Cochlaeus, *Commentaria,* 1, 2; Grisar, *op. cit.,* I, 12.

[52] Grisar, *op. cit.,* III, 706.

[53] *Ausgewählte Werke,* hrsg. von G. Loewe, III, 2, Prag, 1906, 20ff.

[54] *Op. cit.,* 46.   [55] V, 5375-1540.

especially as one of the points which Luther subsequently criticized in the brethren was their effort to make a last of one form fit all feet [56] instead of emphasizing as St. Augustine did the different capacities of mankind to bear burdens.[57]

Whatever difficulties a young scholar of Luther's gifts may have encountered in adjusting himself to a community composed only in part of educated clerics and containing many lay brethren who could not even read or write, they were so well overcome that he left on the minds of contemporary members of the order an impression of exemplary personal conduct. In fact, it seems extremely probable that his novitiate was abridged to a period of six months, instead of the year required by the statutes, and that he made his profession at the end of 1505.[58] On the other hand, we have no evidence that cloister hardships caused Luther to feel personal embitterment against the Augustinian brethren at Erfurt. Never, even under the hardest stress of his rupture with the monastic life, does he complain of unfair treatment among the Eremites. He refers to the Erfurt Congregation often with deep respect and maintained for years after leaving their company a warm friendship with several members holding offices of authority.

The novitiate period can hardly have been passed

[56] WA, XLII, 641; Enarr in Gen., cap. XVII, 9.
[57] WA, XLIV, 705.
[58] A. V. Müller, Theol. Studien und Kritiken, 1921, 283ff.

without giving him a deeper acquaintance with the
Bible. The Erfurt Augustinians had long professed a
desire for "eagerly reading, devoutly hearing and
zealously learning" the Scriptures, and Staupitz had
transferred the ancient exhortation verbally from the
old constitution of 1287 of the German congregations into the new one which he drew up.[59] A quarter of a century later Luther recalls that the brethren
gave him a Bible with a red leather cover and that he
became so familiar with it that he knew the page on
which every verse stood.[60] A less well attested passage of the *Table Talk* states that after his profession
the brethren tried to substitute "scholastic books" for
the Bible, which he, however, found for himself in
the library.[61] In spite of contemporary testimony to
a lack of Bible teaching early in the sixteenth century,
nevertheless nothing is better attested than the opportunities of a young monk of the Augustinian Congregation to become acquainted with Holy Scriptures.

Everything, indeed, points to the fact that despite
the discontent and restlessness which we shall have to
discuss later, the young monk fell in rapidly and
whole-heartedly with cloister discipline, and that this
very discipline in the early years of monastic life fos-
tered a rapid unfolding of inner religious life and a
constant progress in theological scholarship. It fur-

[59] Cap. XV; cf. N. Paulus, *Jahrb. d. Görres Gesellschaft*, Bd. XII, 1891,
31, 2; Scheel, *Luther*, II, 336 Anm. 6.

[60] *TR*, I, 116-1531.   [61] *TR*, V, 5346-1540.

nished him with a training in humility which did
not succeed in tempering the natural independence
and violent obstinacy of his character, yet gave him
patterns of conduct which were of value in promoting self-restraint in later life.

The prior and master of novices must have been
fully satisfied with the ardent young monk, for he
was received into the permanent ranks of the order
when the year of probation was concluded, possibly
even several months before that.[62] Coming from the
solemn consecration of the "profession," a ceremony
girt about with all solemnity as marking the most
momentous step in the monastic ritual, Luther recalls
sarcastically twenty years later that he felt as if he
were now coming forth from baptism as pure as an
innocent child.[63] Learned pens from the Catholic
Church have in recent years contended that no such
idea existed among the Erfurt Augustinians,[64] but
whatever may be the theories of the scholarly interpreters of church doctrine the young monk rose from
his knees after the prayer with which the prior finally
consecrated him to the service of God and the Blessed
Virgin with a vital feeling of purity hitherto unknown to him. With how God-intoxicated a heart
must he have listened to the solemn harmony of ver-
sicles and responses which dedicated to God a soul

[62] Müller advances arguments for this, but does not prove it; cf. *Luthers
Werdegang*, 38, 39.

[63] *WA*, XXXVIII, 147.

[64] Cf. Denifle, *Luther*, 2 Ausg., I, 224.

37193

stripped of self! With what proud content must he have received from prior and brethren the kiss, symbol alike of a life of humility and brotherly love! In this new baptism the burden and torment of sin must, for the moment at least, have rolled away from him.

IV

THEOLOGICAL STUDIES AND SOUL STRUGGLES IN THE CLOISTER

WHEN the ceremony of "profession" was over Luther's career as a civil person seemed ended forever. After the *completorium* had closed the momentous day and the young monk laid himself upon his bed of straw, he could look back upon a life which seemed to offer a singularly adequate preparation for a career of ministry and of sacred studies. Through an organic development during school and university years he had made himself ready for a life of scholarly activity. The profound inner yearnings which culminated in more than one emotional crisis had led him, against the resistance of his other self, unhaltingly to the cloister. The year of rigorous preparation in the ways of discipline and mortification of the flesh must have pushed the memory of all former ambitions into the haze of the past. Inducted into an ancient, sacred order, with the voluntary submission of his own will to its statutes, the sacrifice had now been sealed by sanctions which no contemporary mind was bold enough to affront, for behind them stood the power of Holy Church. The pathway of life lay plain before him, its end visible from his narrow window, beneath which lay in consecrated earth the bones of the brothers who had trodden before him the road of self-denial and suffering. Until he should join them, his duty was to destroy the remnants of sin which the inheritance of Adam bound even to those who had received the "pleasant making grace," and to develop his soul through the love of God and of his neighbor.

For the moment at least a profound peace must have settled upon the young man's heart. Even though the words of the prayer of the cloister chief may still have rung in his ears, warning him of the hardships that lay ahead, he could not but feel the blessed assurance belonging to the select group of those for whom the service of God through love and worship was a profession. Theoretically of course his struggle against sin was still to be carried on, but the step which he had just taken meant to his mind and that of his superiors a guarantee of salvation. "Religion makes its professors like unto the angels, unlike men; yes, in the manner of baptism it recreates the image of God in man," declares the constitution of the Dominican Order of 1507. [1]

---

[1] *"Religio professores suos similes angelis facit, dissimiles hominibus, imo imaginem Dei in homine ad instar baptismi reformat"* (quoted by Müller, *Luthers theologische Quellen*, 1912, 28). Cf. for the age and development of this idea, Scheel, *Luther*, II, 26ff., Anm. 166; W. Braun, *Die Concupiscenz bei Luther im Leben und Lehre*, 1908, 49. Luther returns to the question in his

Nevertheless, perfection must be fought for by monk as well as layman. The attitude of the young Augustinian, "burning with zeal," toward the sacrifices which the ascetic life demanded cannot be measured except by the standards of a time so intoxicated with supernaturalism as was the beginning of the sixteenth century. It cannot be judged either without reference to the exalted impulsiveness of Luther's character. His statements on the subject of his ascetic practices are, as we have seen, many and categorical in character. When on approaching the age of fifty he suffered in health, he ascribed it to the hardships of his life in the cloister. Memories of weakening fasts and of cold that threatened his life are fresh in mind in reviewing his twenty years as monk,[2] and suffering and exhaustion through abstinence and loss of rest and the hardships of monastic duties are again and again the theme in sermons and *Table Talk* in the last decade of his life.[3] Doubt has been thrown on the truth of these statements by Denifle, who has contended that if they are true Martin overstepped the requirements of his order;[4] but monastic literature of the time offers examples enough of severe abstinence on the part of monks who felt conscientiously obliged to go to the extreme

Kleine Antwort auf Herzog Georgen nächstes Buch (WA, XXXVIII, 143, 148); Strohl, *op. cit.*, I, 84.

[2] *WA*, XLV, 670; 482.
[3] *WA*, XLIV, 705; XLIII, 255; cf. 536.
[4] *Luther und das Luthertum*, I, 351ff.

in the mortification of the flesh. Who can doubt that the ardent temperament of young Luther led him to a rigor of renunciation and martyrdom that emulated the example of those ascetics who lived from roots and herbs in the wilderness? Naturally he found in such sacrifices a satisfaction which was quite unintelligible to the aging man, to whom the monastic order was religiously a crime and personally a bitter memory of crushed illusions. The great struggle which culminated ten years later in Wittenberg threw its shadow back to the earliest cloister years and blackened them also. The hardships which we undergo in youth without murmuring, yes, with a certain exhilaration in view of a great ideal, take their color in memory from the success or failure of that ideal, and the middle-aged Luther may well have confused in memory the soul struggles which culminated in the discovery of a new formula for justification a decade later with the ascetic exercises of his order. Thus when he says in 1533 in the most bitterly polemical of his works, the *Brief Answer to Duke George's Next Book,* that if the cloister life had lasted longer he would have tormented himself to death with watching, praying, reading and other tasks, he evidently includes in this arraignment of the monastic life the fearful soul experiences that embittered all his memories of the cloister.[5]

The sources close to the early cloister years indicate

[5] *WA,* XXXVIII, 143, 148.

that the young scholar, who had come to the monastery fired with the desire to secure salvation, accepted the hardships of monastic life after his "profession" with the fiery enthusiasm of a soul gifted with an extraordinary desire to find his God. The only two letters which we have from him the following year, 1507, breathe this spirit. Both are filled with a high sense of pride in his monkhood and are framed in the traditional formulas of monkish humility. The spirit of sacrifice which fires the high purpose of youth floats down to us in a remark in one of Luther's early lectures at Wittenberg, that the novice knew nothing more "jocund" than the monastic life. However repugnant the monkish ideal may have been to him in later life, he accepted it in his youth, as he repeatedly says, with enthusiasm. Thus he recalled that he had counted himself among the pious and just monks,[6] and declares in 1533 that if any son of the cloister could have earned salvation from the monkish calling it would have been he.[7] When in 1521 he speaks of the fear of his father that he would not be able to keep his cloister vow, he shows himself unpricked by conscience for any failure of this kind.[8] "Outwardly," he declares in 1531 in his Commentary on Galatians, "I lived good, just and poor and cared nothing for the world."[9]

[6] WA, XXXIII, 574.　　　　[7] WA, XXXVIII, 143.

[8] WA, VIII, 573.

[9] WA, XL, 1, 137; cf. TR, I, 121-1531; 518-1533.

As life developed within the walls, it was indeed a fierce struggle against sin; and the God-sworn monk, his inward vision sharpened by fear, constantly examined his soul for the mortal sins which might undo the justification of the sacraments. To such a supersensitiveness of conscience may have been added rivalry in the ascetic life, the constant measuring of himself by the example of others. The traditions of the order as they opened before him furnished a severe standard. Luther's early attitude may be measured by the fact that in his paper *On the Monk's Vow* he criticized as a weakening of religious zeal the Dominican restriction of mortal sin to a breach of the three major monastic vows; poverty, chastity and obedience. The young monk must have known, to be sure, of the "discretion" allowed in certain ascetic observances, such as fasting, for he speaks later of those writers who, like Gerson, pleaded for a modification of the severities of the cloister rule.[10] But whatever he may have known or not known of the "mitigations" permissible, to a nature so impulsive the danger lay, as has been stated above, not in neglect but in an excess of zeal. The same sensitiveness of conscience which drove him into the cloister must have led to the severest interpretation of Augustinian duty. Much in the monastic observances must have been left to the individual conscience, and Luther's conscience was an imperious master. As has been

[10] *WA*, XLII, 504-1535; cf. *TR*, II, 1351-1532.

pointed out, after he became district vicar of the
order his correspondence with the heads of the various congregations, in spite of a certain unctuousness
of tone, indicates a rigid interpretation of monastic
law.

At first such questions were far from the young
monk, who still stood in the springtime of religious
life and said to his father, when the latter came to
attend the son's first mass, that his life in the cloister
was such a "fine, quiet and divine life" that at times
he felt as if he were "among the angels." The impression which he made upon the cloister authorities must have been a favorable one, as within a short
time after his profession he was selected for the dignity of the priesthood and for studies in theology.[11]
At least formal approval for reception into the priesthood and for admission to general studies in theology
at the university must have come from the general
vicar, Johann von Staupitz, although there is no evidence that this man, who was to play an important
part in Luther's theological development, came into
personal contact with him at this time. Through his
spectacular conversion Martin was a marked man,
and it is fair to assume that his career at the university
had fixed the attention of the prior and congrega-

[11] If we accept Müller's supposition that Luther's profession took place before Christmas, 1505, his studies may have begun early in 1506. His first
mass was celebrated May 2, 1507. Müller, *L's Werdegang*, 53ff., assumes that
the theological course of studies accompanied the liturgical studies for the
priesthood.

tion on him from the beginning of his novitiate as one who might in future serve the order in high office, and there is reason to believe that his advance from the first orders, through subdeacon and deacon to the final ceremony which delivered into his hands the sacred elements of the mass and clothed him in stole and *casella*, was celebrated at the earliest possible time consistent with the completion of his preliminary studies.

The liturgical and theological training which prepared him for the priesthood had an importance for his development which cannot be overlooked. According to Luther's own statement it was based on Gabriel Biel's canon of the mass, "an excellent book, as I then thought," he declares thirty years later.[12] The eminent author of this interpretation of the Church's great ceremony of propitiation stood in close relation to the Augustinian Order. Both the general vicar, Staupitz, and Luther's teacher of theology, Nathin, had studied under him at Tübingen. Luther recalled many years later that his heart burned within him as he followed this well-accredited guide into his profoundly mystical interpretation of the various sacraments of the church.[13] Here he learned to know God as a God of grace inclined to the worshiper through the commemorative presentation of the bloody sacrifice of Christ, but at the same time he

[12] *TR*, III, 3722-1538; cf. 3146-1532.
[13] *TR*, III, 3722-1538.

was shown God's justice as the foundation of the
moral order. Through a mass of liturgical, canonical
and allegorical material he came face to face with his
full responsibility as ambassador and advocate of
God's beloved church (*nuntius et procurator ecclesiae deo dilectae*).

There is evidence that profound emotions of fear
dominated his thought when the hands of the bishop
were laid upon him in ordination and as a priest
of the Holy Church he was authorized to make
the sacrifice of the mass, to give the true body of
Christ to believers, to hear confession and assign penance, and when the day approached for the great
springtime festival in the life of a young priest, the
celebration of his first mass. The circumstances surrounding this event were of lasting significance for
the soul life of the young religious. Evidence of that
appears in the importance which he himself afterwards attached to the celebration in his sermons and
Table Talk. Here as elsewhere in treating the crisis
of their hero, the early biographers have given rein to
the legend-forming impulse, and their accounts, as
well as the transcripts of the sermons and *Table Talk*
on which they are based, embellish the celebration
with dramatic incidents which are in part improbable
and in part self-contradictory.[14] Aside from such
fantastic details, the sources show that in the memory

[14] *Enarratio in Genesin* (WA, XLIII, 382); *TR*, II, 1558-1532; III, 3556a-
1537; cf. 3556b; V, 5357-1540; *TR*, IV, 4174, and Müller, *Werdegang*, 71.

of the aging reformer the occasion was girt about with an extraordinarily keen realization of the power and responsibilities of the priesthood.

The celebration of mass by a young priest of Luther's intensity of temperament must have accelerated greatly the growth of the fears and anxieties which were already assailing him or were to assail him with increasing force during the years immediately following. Heretofore he had approached the God of Law through the mediation of the Virgin or one of the saints; now for the first time he realized what it meant to stand in the living Presence. The reality of God must then have thrust itself upon him with stunning force, and he remembered a generation later the anxiety which beset him lest he might by some lapse of memory or carelessness bring himself into mortal sin in the sacred office, for there rang in his ears the solemn warning of his manual of instruction, Biel, on this point.[15]

Significant is an incident which may belong to this time and which made a deep impression upon the young priest. The celebration of the mass had led to a reconciliation with his father.[16] In answer to the son's explanation that he had been called to the cloister by a terror from heaven, the old miner burst out in violent indignation: "What if it were only a delusion of Satan?" Twice in the great year of his

---

[15] *Von der Winkelmesse* (EA, XXXI, 331-1532); cf. *TR*, IV, 4174-1538.
[16] *TR*, I, 623, 881-1533; III, 3556-1537.

appearance before the Diet of Worms Luther recalls the old man's remark.[17] The words of the father remained with all the force of the mythology of early youth, nestled in his heart as an indestructible, tormenting point of doubt.[18]

Any investigation of the development of Luther's religious character in the years directly following his admission to the monastic order and his consecration as priest must take two factors into consideration: the inner psychological experiences which marked the progress of his soul life, and the theological studies which occupied him intensely during this period. Luther was, of course, two beings—a young man struggling to adjust his ideas of God to the changing inner experiences of life, and a theological student seeking in the Scriptures and in scholarly works formulas for Christian faith. The two are interlocked in any review of his development. The crisis of soul through which he passed, and to which he returned again and again in later years with shuddering, grew out of a temperament which, as we have seen, fired religious experiences to a singular intensity. This intense emotional nature reacted sharply to his theological studies, feeding upon the theories of grace in patristic and scholastic literature and seeking to adapt them to meet demands of the soul. On the other

[17] *Enders*, III, 225; *WA*, VIII, 573ff.
[18] He recalls them in a sermon three years before his death (*WA*, XLIX, 322).

hand, his studies stimulated religious experience and finally swung open the doors leading to an assurance of personal salvation. It cannot be overlooked that, in spite of its many associations with political, economic and educational movements, the Reformation thus grew out of theological sources and had its beginning in a theological position of Martin Luther.

But Luther was no historically minded theologian, nor were the theories which he defended mere intellectual propositions. They were the result of experiences in which the ideas of the Church Fathers became his own through stages of intense suffering, for he sought in Church Father and scholast, not that which might satisfy intellectual curiosity or aid in the erection of a system of theological thought, but that which could serve as a rock of refuge in the storms of fear of death and eternal pain which visited him. The discovery of theological concepts, on the other hand, first fanned the emotional flame into a blaze and then brought the faith which was both emotionally and intellectually satisfying. It is that which gives to the cloister years their intense interest and invests with so much importance the studies of patristic and scholastic authority in the period immediately following his "profession."

The first stage of these studies covers the period until his first departure for Wittenberg in 1508. When theological studies began, the sources do not say, but much speaks for the hypothesis that they had

an earlier beginning than scholars have heretofore assigned to them and that they may have covered three
of the three and one-half years which intervened between the beginning of his novitiate and the transfer
to Wittenberg.[19]　He was forthwith to enter a period
of preparation for service in the teacher's chair.
There is evidence, as has been stated, that his remarkable conversion had made him a marked man in his
cloister, and it is a possible, although not a necessary
deduction from the sources, that the general vicar
Staupitz had already had his attention called to one
who, besides wearing the nimbus of the miraculous,
was also in all probability marked as a scholar of brilliant promise.[20]　The duty of study was, like the call
to the priesthood and every other task in conventual
life, not a matter of individual initiative, but lay, by
the constitution of the order, in the hands of the
general vicar or the general chapter of the congregation; and no head of a congregation intent on ful-
filling what was avowedly a major purpose of the
Augustinians, the cultivation of scholarship, could
have overlooked the young master of arts.

The Saxon-Thuringian province of the Order of
the Eremites maintained at Erfurt, as afterwards at
Wittenberg, an institute of higher study (*Studium
generale*).　That at Erfurt had already a history of
one hundred years when Luther entered the Congregation.[21]　Like similar institutes at the Franciscan and

[19] *Luther's Werdegang*, 54.　[20] *Ibid.*, 45, 53ff.　[21] Oergel, *op. cit.*, 54ff.

Dominican establishments in the city, the general study at the Augustinian convent was closely interlocked with the university. Indeed, at the time of Luther's residence in the cloister the Augustinians seem to have furnished the leading teachers in the university theological faculty; and the brothers carried on their studies freely at the university. A succession of men who combined a strictly observant type of mind with great theological scholarship held these positions in the years of Luther's residence.

Under their direction life can have had few leisure moments for him. The constitution of the order provided that the duties of the choir and of other liturgical exercises and theological study must go together hand in hand without damage to either.[22] The candidate for the baccalaureate in Bible studies must hear lectures on the whole of the *Sentences* of Peter Lombard, and we may assume that Luther, as was customary in the late medieval university, began his studies with this work, which supplied the dogmatic basis for Christian theology.[23] In addition, he was obliged to attend an exegetical course on at least one of the books of the Old and one of the New Testament. He must have found time for other reading as well, for we know from his marginal notes on Lombard, when he began to lecture on him two years later, that he was already familiar with Gabriel Biel's commentary on the great dogmatist. The Erfurt

[22] Chapter 36.   [23] Denifle-Chatelain, *Chartularium*, II, 688.

monastery, as Luther says in a letter to his friend
Lang in 1516,[24] was given over to "Gabrielismus,"
and for years to come the young theologian absorbed
into himself the ideas of the Tübingen scholar.[25]

In Biel he found the same "modernist" ideas which
he had learned to know before his entry into the convent and which were as strongly held in the convent
as by his teachers at the university.[26]   So thoroughly
was he inoculated with modernist conceptions that it
is very doubtful if he ever read intelligently or understood the father of scholastic philosophy, the
"divine" Thomas Aquinas,[27] whom he criticizes later
so vigorously for having been led astray by metaphysics.[28]   Not the Celestial Father but William of
Occam was now, as before, his philosophical-theo-
logical leader and saturated his thought.   It is possible that he read at this time another great scholast,
Duns Scotus, whose work on the third book of Lombard's *Sentences* remained thirty years later a forceful
memory.[29]   But his very earliest lectures show him
strongly prejudiced against the whole school of
Realists.[30]   These studies in theology reburnished
metaphysical and dialectical faculties which he had
begun to exercise at the university.

[24] *Enders*, I, 55.
[25] Melanchthon says that Luther almost knew the work by heart (*Corpus Ref.*, VI, 159).
[26] Cf. *WA*, VI, 195, 600.   [27] Denifle, *op. cit.*, I, 522, 573.
[28] *TR*, III, 3722.
[29] *TR*, IV, 5009; III, 3722-1538; cf. *WA*, II, 403.   [30] *WA*, IX, 83.

It is hard to see how the arid subtleties of the school-men could have fired the zeal of a young monk or satisfied an imagination which yearned, as he tells us later, to come into contact with "some good man." They must have been joined to a greater extent than apologistic tradition admits with a study of the Bible itself. Early biographers, as has been pointed out, assumed an ignorance regarding the Bible in Luther's day which is clearly not in accord with the facts. Thus, Mathesius says that after Martin had become a priest he had to give up the Bible and read scholastic and philosophical works, but that he hid himself in the library as often as he could and read the Bible. There is nothing in the primary sources to support this and it is quite contrary to the statutes of the Augustinian Order, which, as we have seen, required the novice to read and learn the Bible. Furthermore, the early part of the theological course at the university consisted of exegetical lectures on books of the Old and the New Testament. It is doubtful, of course, if the scholars who directed Luther's theological studies had anything like the interest in Biblical interpretation which they brought to the dogmatic courses, but even so the young student must have found something in the exegetical courses which pulsed with life, for as a doctor of philosophy at Wittenberg a few years later he shows in his earliest lectures on the Psalms and Romans a maturity of method in this side of theological study which he subsequently develops to the point of genius.

Although we have no reason to suppose that he did not have opportunity for the study of the Bible, it is certain that neither his Biblical courses nor those on Lombard's dogmatics nor any of the other hair-spun theories of the theologians brought him peace. The inner history of his soul struggles during this early period of theological study cannot be told, of course. The outer events of his life in the five years following his consecration as priest may be traced with a fair degree of accuracy. They include his early study of theology at Erfurt, his year as student and teacher at Wittenberg and the continuation of this activity at Erfurt, his journey to Rome and final removal to Wittenberg, when he becomes professor of Bible and district vicar of his order. From the time when his lectures at Erfurt began (1509) the young instructor's own notes enable us to mark the gradual widening of his reading and the winning of an independent standpoint and the crystallization of new ideas regarding justification and the remission of sins. But for the earlier period no contemporary sources are open to us and we are dependent on later references in sermons and particularly in passages in the *Table Talk*, when Luther chattered on earlier cloister reminiscences with the garrulity of middle age. Then many soul experiences were no longer clear, and many took color from the overpowering events that followed each other so closely after 1517. All are conveyed to us through the medium of a younger generation to which cloister life was unknown. To the student of Luther, as to Luther himself as he looked back on his life from the high point of the middle years, the fears and the doubts and the anguish of soul which assailed him all form parts of one great experience which filled the decade from 1507 to 1517.

Denifle, who led the most active Catholic attack on Luther in the early years of the twentieth century, denied the reality of such crises in Luther's religious development. No part of the bellicose Dominican's attack has been more bitterly resented by Protestant apologists, for here he attempted to destroy one of the dearest traditions of Protestantism. Indeed, it seems impossible to read the sources with open mind and not experience the genuineness of Luther's testimony on this point.[31] It would be more correct, however, to speak of a *series* of crises, all of them parts of the same struggle, whether taking place in his cell at Erfurt or in the Black Tower at Wittenberg, a struggle between what he heard from his teachers and cloister elders or read in Biel and Scotus and what he found in independent study of the Fathers and the Bible, illuminated by his own conscience.

[31] Strohl, *L'évolution réligieuse de Luther,* lists ten pages of references to these experiences, taken from Luther's sermons, letters and *Table Talk.*

At times there was a crisis when Luther's tormented soul sought in vain for an answer; at others a wise word of his confessor or superior pointed the way to a Bible text or gave a new direction to his thought, and this for the moment brought comfort. These rays of light remained precious in his mind and the sane and godly men who shed them were unforgettable. They all helped him in a process which went steadily onward through the ferment of young manhood and eventually brought forth a new theology.

After 1509, when we begin to have contemporary notes, followed three years later by letters, lectures and sermons, the development of his religious ideas appears organic rather than sudden and catastrophic. We do not find in these sources traces of the dramatic features which the sixteenth-century biographers, and to some extent the aging reformer himself, wove around his early religious development. This does not justify us in doubting, however, that the years for which we have no contemporary documents, the years immediately following his consecration as priest, were marked by an unusual restlessness of soul. The evidence for this is so categorical that it cannot be brushed aside. This anguish of mind may be explained in part by the life of the monk itself, with the melancholy begotten of hardships, loneliness and constant study, unrelieved by diversion. This depression was recognized by the monks themselves, as

Luther tells us, as "a bath of melancholy prepared by the devil," [32] and he was sure that the devil seeks to bring earnest Christians to a fall thereby.[33] He was, as later life shows, neither of a scholastic nor contemplative type of mind, and was suited rather to the active struggles of the world outside than the peculiar routine of the cloister. It is well documented for later years that he was subject to fits of acute depression, certainly not independent of physical causes, and these nerve crises were associated with religious experiences, some of them of crucial character. His doubts and fears, which as he remembered in middle life had caused him in his cloister years to encounter continually ever and again the temptation to melancholy,[34] still assailed him long after he had seen a reformed church rise under his guidance.[35] These "temptations" of doubt and fear beset him with such suddenness and intensity in the cloister that their memory burned itself into his soul and expressed itself in constant and dramatic expressions in his letters and *Table Talk*.[36] Such crises, which are indeed as unfathomable to the investigator as the profound depths of personality are everywhere, he suffered from chronic sensitiveness of conscience. In his earlier days in the cloister this drove him constantly to

[32] *TR*, I, 455.

[33] Letter to Weller, 1530 (*Enders*, VIII, 159).

[34] *TR*, III, 3593-1537.

[35] *TR*, I, 461; cf. Melanchthon, *Corp. Ref.*, VI, 158.

[36] *TR*, I. 122, 352, 461, 518, 979, etc.

the confessional,[37] where he tried to force himself to become contrite and could not.[38]

Out of such anguished hours as these came the young theologian's rejection of scholastic theology, particularly the theories of the "modernists" as a means of satisfying his longing for peace of soul. It is necessary therefore to understand, so far as the sources permit, the actual nature of the "temptations" which assailed him.

Luther had entered the cloister with the hope of winning a gracious God. At the beginning of his monastic life he may well have found satisfaction in the thought that he had won acceptance by God through his sacrifice. He knew, as he informs us repeatedly in later years, that he stood under the protection of the guarantees of his order and could reckon on the intercession of the saints in his behalf,[39] and he directed his prayers, he says, not to Christ, but to St. George and others.[40] Grace could be obtained, however, only through complete repentance for sin, and he never could be sure that he had repented completely.[41] His conscience found no repose because it was not appeased by his works.[42] God appeared to him as a God of Justice and he trembled when he read from the Psalter, "Redeem me through

[37] *TR*, I, 122-1531.

[38] *Enarr. Psalm (EA, Ex. opp. lat.*, XIX, 100 [1532]).

[39] *WA*, XLVI, 663-1537; XLVII, 461, 589, etc.

[40] *WA*, XLVII, 461.   [41] *WA*, I, 321.

[42] *Enarr. in Gen. (WA*, XLIII, 536-1540-42).

Thy justice (Ps. xxxi. 2)," having in mind only the punitive justice of God, which he felt that he could never satisfy.[43]

As the young monk's theological studies opened, he heard repeated from the theological standpoint the same ideas regarding the freedom of the will and the powers of the intellectual man with his ethical possibilities and limitations as he had learned in his philosophical lectures at the university before his entry into the monastery. His mind was active and constructive rather than metaphysical. He never carried his theological scholarship to a point where he could have been regarded as deeply learned. His nature prompted him to seize a few basic ideas and develop them into principles of action. Neither in Erfurt nor elsewhere did he have the time or guidance to enable him to master the history of dogma, but he could only take such ideas as were presented in the works which he read with their interpretation in the lectures which he heard, and give them a new direction in accordance with his genius. As we have seen, the entire atmosphere of Erfurt was that of the Nominalist theology, and Luther, as Denifle has shown,[44] quite misunderstood the Thomistic interpretation of divine grace and its relation to the freedom of the will.[45]

The theology which he did receive and understand

[43] *TR*, V, 5247.   [44] *Op. cit.*, I, 2, 543 ff.
[45] Cf. *Enders*, II, 109.

was that of William of Occam.[46] "I am of Occam's party," he declares several years later,[47] and he calls Occam "the chief and most clever of the schoolmen."[48] How much he himself read of Occam's works in Erfurt and later, it is impossible to say, though it has been asserted that he knew him chiefly through Biel.[49] In his lectures at Wittenberg in 1516 we find him standing on Occam's position with regard to the preparation for God's grace.[50] Three years later in reviewing the theology which he had been taught, he declares that he learned that man can do his own part to obtain grace, removing the obstacles opposed to it; that he can observe the divine commandments according to their substance; that in the work of salvation the will is free to choose and capable by its natural forces of loving God above everything.[51] These are ideas of Occam. In place of a series of supernatural interferences which the Thomists taught, Occam presents the theory that man prepares himself for saving grace by voluntarist forces of his own. Whoever exerts all the powers that are in him (*quod in se est*) may receive this grace. Thus man "entices" God, as Luther expresses

---

[46] For a good summary of the medieval theories of grace cf. Strohl, *op. cit.*, I, 90 ff.

[47] *WA*, VI, 600; cf. VI, 193 and above.

[48] *WA*, VI, 183.

[49] Grisar, *op. cit.*, I, 104.

[50] Letter to Lang, 1516; Enders, I, 55; cf. Scheel, *SchrVfRG*, C, 125 ff.

[51] Commentary on Galatians (*WA*, II, 401-1519).

it in his lectures; man draws near to God by loving him above everything, and as soon as this occurs, God pours grace into his heart.[52] The works of man then become just, but even then they can claim no merit toward salvation unless God accepts them, and this acceptance depends altogether on the sovereign and arbitrary will of God.

It is clear then that the Occamists did not believe that works of themselves make men just, a statement which Luther unhesitatingly condemns in his lectures on Romans. With Occam, the great bridge between the "disposition" through moral, individual acts which the Middle Ages found in the ethics of Aristotle and the acceptance by God comes through the arbitrary will of God. The human will, in Occam's theory, must exert itself to earn and deserve justification, but that is not enough. For the works done even in a state of grace have no merit in themselves but merely through their acceptance by God. The heavenly reward must be earned, but supernatural grace arbitrarily bestowed alone can avail to entitle man's efforts to salvation.

This, then, was the theory of salvation which Luther received at Erfurt and which formed in later years the object of his attack. The airy structure is a curious mixture of human rationalism and of divine voluntarism. Both sides added elements to the despair which assailed Luther in his cloister crises. God

[52] WA, IV, 262.

and Christ are judges, judging men according to their works. Man must therefore do his best, but how could the young monk be sure that he was doing his best? "When I saw Christ," he states in his violent way many years afterwards, "it seemed to me as if I were seeing the devil. For that reason one said, 'Dear Mary, pray thy dear son for me and still his wrath.' " [53] Sin lurked on every side, mortal sin, perhaps, that could be removed only by confession and absolution. For that reason he confessed so often. But what avail were confessions when every movement of evil desire, anger, hatred, etc., *concupiscence* as Luther defines it, seemed to him to destroy his salvation.[54] It was in vain he had entered the monastery, for all his good works were useless. As late as 1515 in his lectures on Romans he declares that he felt often that he must despair of God, and that whenever he thought of the test that lay before him at the end of life his heart trembled and shook. How could God be merciful to him? [55]

To these doubts of his finding grace at the hands of a just God was added the dreadful uncertainty derived from the other side of the Occamist theory, the fear that his works, even though done under grace, might nevertheless fail of acceptance by God. This, which in the last analysis includes the dogma of pre-

[53] *WA*, XLV, 86.　　　　[54] *WA*, XL, 2, 92.
[55] Cf. *Kleine Antwort auf Herzog Georgen nächstes Buch* (*WA*, XXXVIII, 148-1533).

destination, must have come to Luther's attention early in his theological studies. His marginal notes on Lombard's *Sentences*, written in 1509, the year after his return to Erfurt from Wittenberg, show that this thought already occupied his mind.[56] Perhaps the supreme "temptation" of the early years of theological study came from this subject, for long years afterwards he had not shaken himself free from feelings of anguish regarding it. "When I get to thinking of this," he declares in 1532, "I forget all that God and Christ are and come to the point where God is a villain . . . where the *laudate* ceases and the *blasphemate* begins." [57]

Such hours of anguish of soul were undoubtedly interrupted by periods in which the young student of theology found contentment and happiness in the performance of liturgical duties and submission to the rigors of ascetic discipline, in the thought that his works had, as Master Occam taught, received acceptance with God through His free choice. There were many days when, as he puts it later, he trusted in the holiness of good works.[58] There were periods also of a mystic stilling of the will which made him feel that he had found God. In the writings of Bonaventure he declared that he sought the path to the union of the soul with God through the joining of the intellect

[56] *WA*, IX, 57.

[57] *TR*, II, 2654; *WA*, II, 688; V, 620ff. Cf. also the *Praefatio* of 1545 (*EA, Opp. lat. var. arg.*, I, 22) and *TR*, I, 1009, 1017.

[58] *WA*, XLIX, 602-1544, etc.

and the will.[59] At times he exults in the search for God along mystic, theosophical paths. In later, more rationalistic years he declared that he had once belonged to the school of mystics and thought himself among the angels, when in reality he was among devils.[60] Then again in moments of despair, as he recollected in later years, the condemnatory justice of God seemed to him like a thunderbolt launched into his conscience.[61]

In such crises help would come from friends. Thus Melanchthon tells of an old man in the Congregation in Erfurt who called his attention to a passage from St. Bernard, where the latter reminds us that in saying the Apostles' Creed, "I believe," each one of us must believe that God has overcome his sins.[62] Melanchthon adds that the remark made a lasting impression on Luther, who recognized now for the first time the emptiness of the current ideas of divine grace. The story finds confirmation in Luther's use of this quotation from St. Bernard in his lectures on Romans in 1515 in discussing the certainty of the forgiveness of sins.[63] Indeed Luther's acquaintance with St. Bernard is documented by the frequent use of him which Müller has found in the first lecture on Psalms,[64]

[59] TR, I, 644-1533.

[60] Enarr. in Ies., Cap. IX-1543 (EA, Ex. opp. lat., XXIII, 401).

[61] TR, II, 1681-1532; III, 3232; IV, 4007-1538.

[62] Corp. Ref., VI, 159.   [63] Ficker, 2, 197, 23ff.

[64] Müller has also pointed out, pp. 84ff., that Luther might have found much in Bernard as a contrast to the Scotist-Occamist theology of his teachers: the complete insufficiency of the natural powers of man.

and by the praise which Luther bestows upon him in his *Table Talk* and sermons.[65] The unclearness of the early biographers on the formation of Luther's early theological notions [66] is no doubt due to a haziness of memory on the part of Luther himself, to whom his road to the certain assurance of salvation, as he looked back on it, was wrapped in darkness, broken only by occasional flashes of light.

Such a flash of light from above he recalls in 1532 in his lectures on Psalms. At a time, he tells us, when the pangs of conscience could not be healed by absolution, his confessor said to him, "Do you not know, my son, that the Lord himself bids us hope?" [67] Many a time confession and the service of the mass must have brought him real relief: he records this in his lectures on Romans [68] and elsewhere.[69] There were also times, as he states a few years later in the lectures on Romans, when he felt the certainty of grace,[70] as well as others, when, as he penitently says in 1516 and repeats bitterly in middle life, he could perform miracles in God's name to make men holy "and devour death and the devil." [71]

St. Bernard's attacks on human righteousness pointed the way to Augustine and the Bible, and possibly the reading of the great patron of his order had

[65] *TR*, I, 872; *WA*, VIII, 601; XLVI, 782-1537; XLVII, 109-1538.
[66] Scheel, *Luther*, II, 137.
[67] *WA*, XI, 2, 411.   [68] *Ficker*, 2, 109.
[69] *TR*, III, 2935b-1535.   [70] *Ficker*, 2, 273.
[71] Letter to Spenlein, April 8, 1516 (*Enders*, I, 29); *WA*, XXXVIII, 148.

already begun thus early. Augustinian in his thought was also Gerson, whom Luther calls his counselor. The former rector of the University of Paris, whose attitude in defense of the rights of the Council against the Pope was later to occupy Luther's attention at a great crisis in his life, was a widely read author of consolatory works addressed to souls seized by the terrors of God's judgments.[72] He exhorted them not to trust in works. God loves souls which despair of themselves and put their trust in Him. "Attaining to hope through despair," from Gerson's *De consolatione theologiæ,* contains a theology dear to Luther in his lectures on Romans. It was also in this work of Gerson's that the old cloister brother found the sentence with which he comforted the young monk regarding God's command to us to hope,[73] a passage which continued to comfort Luther in later years, as Melanchthon tells us. Another passage from the Paris theologian, quoted from Proverbs, xviii, 17, "*Justus in principio accusator est sui,*" becomes a winged word in the earlier lecture courses, which contain many expressions from Gerson stressing the necessity that man should humiliate himself in the dust in order to find grace.[74]

Perhaps through this comforter Luther found his

[72] *TR,* I, 979; II, 1351; cf. Müller, *Luthers Werdegang,* 76ff.; Strohl, *L'évolution réligieuse de Luther,* 108.

[73] *Deus mille locis scripturae sacrae praecipit ut speres in Deo,* Col. 21; cf. Müller, *Luthers Werdegang,* 79ff.

[74] Cf. Strohl, *op. cit.,* 109.

way at this time to another Paris theologian whom he names among those who gave him strength, William of Paris, also well known in Germany.[75] In such counselors he found Christ and His wounds held up as the only secure basis for hope, as well as the demand that faith must precede the reception of the sacrament of penance.

That an acquaintance with these theological consoling spirits goes well back into the early Erfurt period is an hypothesis which is supported by the remarkable readiness with which Luther refers to St. Bernard and Gerson in his lectures on Psalms in 1513-14. They brought consolation in hours of darkness and hope in the passion of despair. They implanted suggestions which were later to ripen under the influence of Augustine and St. Paul. They were not strong enough to overthrow the Nominalist theory, but they had at least begun to undermine it before Luther's departure for Wittenberg. As yet his faith in Holy Church and Pope were unshaken; indeed, he assures us in the sketch of his development prepared in the last year of his life that they remained unshaken for twelve years after he entered the Augustinian cloister.[76] He was ready to bring straw and wood for burning heretics like Huss, or at least would have stood by with assenting heart, as he tells us later.[77] He was one with his teacher Biel in regard-

[75] TR, II, 1351; cf. Müller, Luthers Werdegang, 82.
[76] EA, Opp. lat. var. arg. I, 16.   [77] WA, XL, 1, 138.

ing the Pope as the successor of St. Peter and the center from which all ecclesiastical power was derived. In short, he was "entirely submerged in the dogma of the papacy."

V

AUGUSTINE AND THE FIRST THEOLOGICAL LECTURES

THE years of theological study which intervened between Luther's profession as monk and his first transfer to Wittenberg in 1508 must have been years of intense mental activity. Such hours as could be spared from the obligatory liturgical duties and devotional exercises, which have been calculated at six hours per day,[1] must have been given over to severe studies; and such hours of exemption as fell to him as a student from the stern requirements of the cloister must have been occupied in the same way. These studies, as we have seen, embraced lectures at the university, possibly also in the convent, given by masters of arts on the Bible and on the great source-book of dogma, the *Sentences* of Peter Lombard.

The development of theological studies in the Middle Ages had assigned to the great systematist of the scholastic world the place of honor in clerical education. The study of the Fathers had been well-nigh forced out of the picture in the thirteenth cen-

[1] *Luthers Werdegang,* 28 ff.

tury,[2] and Aristotle dominated the schools so completely that exegetical studies fell into the background. Church dogma was built up not from the Scriptures but from the analytical foundation of Lombard's *Sentences,* although certain books of the Bible formed the subject of lectures. It is characteristic for the system prevailing in Luther's youth that the young monk was promoted early to the grade of bachelor in the Bible (*biblicus baccalaureus*) and lectured on the Bible, while further studies were necessary before he could undertake to expound the system of Christian faith as set forth in Lombard.[3]

Whatever studies were required of him, however, he must have fulfilled them with the same success that had marked his academic career from the first and which marked him throughout life as an academic personality. In the fall of 1508, as he was approaching the first objective of his theological course, the baccalaureate in Bible, he was suddenly transferred to the convent of his order in Wittenberg,[4] so suddenly that even his intimate friends did not know of it. The reasons for this can only be surmised. The university at Wittenberg was at that time scarcely six years old, and in its struggle for growth in the face of the rivalry of Leipsic and Erfurt the little cloister of Wittenberg Augustinians under the general vicar,

[2] Denifle, *Universitäten des Mittelalters,* I, 759, Anm.
[3] Müller, *Luthers Werdegang,* 61.
[4] Letter to Braun, March 17, 1509 (*Enders,* I, 5).

Staupitz played an important rôle. University and cloister studies must have formed more nearly one unified body than was the case at Erfurt, for the university depended for its support on ecclesiastical foundations. The personnel and masters of instruction of the university were very largely supported by two institutions in the city—All Saints Church and the Augustinian monastery. Staupitz, who had become in 1503 head of the reformed Augustinian Eremites, was professor of Bible and dean of the theological faculty, and the Augustinian conventual house was the first place of instruction. There is no possible doubt that the young scholar, whose career at the university must have been set in further relief by his unusual spiritual experiences, had already attracted the attention of Staupitz and owed his transfer to the general vicar's choice. More regarding the relations between the two will be said below.

Whatever the circumstances of his transfer, Luther was at once required to put at the service of the cloister and university the studies in the Aristotelian philosophy which had formed so essential a part of his training in his pre-monkish days. His duties as teacher included lectures on moral philosophy, probably the interpretation of the *Nicomachean Ethics* of Aristotle.[5] The studies in philosophy which this teaching entailed were an unwelcome distraction from the pursuit of theology, to which he had fully given

[5] Oergel, *op. cit.*, 110.

his heart as the true "kernel of the nut." Whatever the demands were, they were fulfilled in the shortest time possible, and on March 9, 1509, Luther was admitted to his baccalaureate in Bible.[6]

New responsibilities now came upon him. He must give "cursory" lectures on Holy Scriptures without being able to give up those on philosophy, as it appears. After one semester he applied for the second theological degree, that of sententiarius, held his public disputation, and was preparing for his initial lecture when another sudden summons recalled him to his mother cloister in Erfurt. Here, after some delay, he received his degree and proceeded to expound the system of theology as set forth by Lombard.

The Wittenberg year must have been a period of rapid soul development. His studies in theology had advanced to a point where they enabled him to take a wide view of the dogmas of the church and perhaps a more objective view of his own difficulties in the struggle to adjust his conscience to traditional teaching. It seems probable also that during this year the young monk came into terms of intimate association with the man whom he names on many occasions as

[6] Müller points out that, although the Wittenberg statutes guaranteed to a member of the religious orders a shortening of the required five-year period of study, the university records show that Luther was not presented for his first degree by his order, and finds support in this for argument that Luther had already been a student of theology for a much longer time than previous Luther investigators have assumed (cf. Luthers Werdegang, 55). This is highly probable, although the evidence is not conclusive. In any event there must have been some shortening of the statutory period of preparation.

the one who set him on the path to peace of conscience. This was Johann von Staupitz, the head of the Reformed Congregation of Augustine Eremites and one of the fathers of the new university. Of this forceful churchman, one of those whom association with Luther has kept in well-deserved remembrance by later generations, not much is known, and the research which in recent years has thrown so much additional light on the early development of Luther has been able to add little to our knowledge. An unprinted manuscript of his sermons in the Munich University library and a dissertation published in Tübingen indicate energy and scholarship and the union of intellectual ability and sound judgment which contemporaries praised in him. This was shown further by his success in promoting the two ideals of the Augustinian Order, devotion to a strict observance of the Rule and an enthusiasm for scholarship. Such a man must have won early the loyalty of a brilliant young academician like Luther.

Just when Luther met this man, who was to become such an important factor in his outer as well as inner life, cannot be said with certainty. If we may trust his recollections many years later, he knew him in Erfurt, for he recalls a conversation there in which Staupitz defended the severity of God's judgment as saving the righteous from evil men.[7]   As we have

[7] *TR*, I, 94-1531.

seen, Staupitz must have given at least formal approval to Luther's reception into the convent.[8] An old tradition in Protestant Germany claims that Luther discovered the Pauline gospel in Erfurt and through Staupitz. The brilliant young monk, who was a marked man among his fellows both in scholarship and soul history, may well have attracted the attention of the general vicar in the latter's search for recruits for the general study at Wittenberg, and it is fair to assume that, in the intimacy of the small Wittenberg cloister, with their unity of academic interest, relations of sympathetic understanding grew up between them. Luther found in Staupitz a power of a sympathy and a depth of understanding to which he refers again and again. Ten years later when the strife over indulgences was hottest, Luther in transmitting his famous *Resolutions* on indulgences to Staupitz writes a dedicatory letter, a memorable document, in which he makes a sort of general confession to a spiritual father. In this he recalls the help which the general vicar gave him in a great crisis.[9] He declares that Staupitz told him that true repentance commences with the love of the justice of God: that which according to others is the climax and end of repentance was thus shown as its beginning. Again in 1523, Luther writes Staupitz that from him "first the light of the gospel began to shine through the

[8] *Constitutio*, Chap. XVI; cf. Müller, *Luthers Werdegang*, 16ff.
[9] Letter of May 30, 1518 (*Enders*, I, 196).

darkness into my heart." [10]   Again, four years before
his death, Luther writes Albrecht von Mansfeld that
he would have been long in hell if God, through Doctor Staupitz, had not helped him out.[11]   Clear down
to 1545, in a lecture, he refers to Staupitz in terms
of great affection.[12]   In spite of the fact that Staupitz
lived and died a faithful Catholic and that Luther
in the day of bitter polemics in 1525 criticized him
for coldness and lack of ardor,[13] he comes back in his
Table Talk again and again to the sound and helpful
advice given him by the general vicar and its value
to him in the agony of soul before he had yet worked
out his theological views.   He affirms that Staupitz
"began the gospel doctrine" which demands that we
look upon the man Christ Jesus.[14]   When doubts assailed him as to whether God is friendly to him, it is
to Staupitz that he makes confession.[15]   When the
ever-recurring temptations beset him, Staupitz refers
him to Gerson [16] and points out to him that such
doubts are necessary for his development.[17]

It is not possible to say just how the experienced
and practical theologian helped the ardent young
monk in his soul battles in the earlier years of their
association.   He probably lacked the ability to see

[10] *Enders*, IV, 231.
[11] Letter of Feb. 23, 1542 (*Enders*, XIV, 189).
[12] Köstlin-Kamerau, *Luther*, I, 71.
[13] Letter to Link (*Enders*, V, 122).
[14] *TR*, I, 526; cf. I, 173.   [16] *TR*, II, 1288-1531.
[15] *TR*, I, 518.   [17] *TR*, I, 141-1531; also I, 518.

into the fiery depths of the young professor's soul, but he offered the support of a practical Christian who had fought his own way to soul peace. He had, as he told Luther, once tried to become a saint, but would try it no more. He had deceived God too long: "It did not do any good." [18] Much speaks for the suggestion that Staupitz showed the young monk a way out of his despondency over the Occamist ideas of repentance. Martin had once tried to persuade himself that he had the final *habitus*, the love of God, but the full repentance which it demanded had become a bitter word for him. Did he really have this absolutely full repentance for sin? Here, he declares, Staupitz came to his aid and showed him that repentance is not, as Luther had been taught, a series of steps by which a disposition is created enabling us to receive the various degrees of grace, crowned finally by the *caritas*, the selfless love of God. God does not offer us salvation bit by bit as we fit ourselves for it. The *caritas* stands at the *beginning* of repentance and not at its end. These words, says Luther in his prefatory letter to the *Resolutions*, stuck in him "like a sharp arrow," [19] and he found them confirmed in Holy Writ. From now on nothing was so pleasant to him as repentance. Henceforth he could feel that God went with him on the path of penance for sin. Henceforth all struggling and agony for full repentance were useless, for a friendly

[18] *TR*, IV, 4868, 1540.   [19] *Enders*, I, 196.

and helpful God followed him with His love. It is not strange that the voice of Staupitz rang to him in "heavenly tones."

No burden lay so heavy upon Luther's soul as the dogma of predestination. Here also the general vicar, who had probably comforted many young men broken in the conflict with the metaphysical theories of scholastic theology, lifted a leaden weight from his young colleague's heart. Like a practical missionary, he pointed him to the wounds of Christ, whom God predestines to suffer for our sins,[20] a hint which Luther later passes on to his students in his lectures on Romans.[21] Thus, with the practiced hand of a realist, Staupitz took the sufferer out of himself and the vicious circle of his own thoughts and directed him to the visible love of God. It was not given to the older man to understand the ardent soul of the young monk, battling with a vivid sense of the reality of sin. As an earnest, practical mystic, and a sympathetic personality he applied the healing casuistry of monkish practice to Luther's suffering and opened Martin's eyes to a simpler conception of grace than he had thus far held.[22]

[20] *TR*, II, 1490, 1820; II, 2654a&b-1532; cf. *TR*, II, 1532.

[21] *Ficker*, 2, 226, 69.

[22] This seems to me to be all that can be claimed for Staupitz' influence on Luther. I share the opinion of Jundt that it was his therapeutic religious personality, rather than the novelty of his theological ideas, that was of such beneficent effect on Luther. Seeberg holds that Luther received from the general vicar the ideas (1) that repentance consists in the love of God, (2) that God leads us to this repentance in revealing Himself to us by the work

The reason why the young sententiarius was transferred back to Erfurt just as he was about to give his
initial lecture at Wittenberg [23] can only be imagined.
Müller [24] calls attention to the fact that seven years
later, after five years' uninterrupted residence in
Wittenberg, Luther is still regarded as a son (*filius*)
of the Erfurt cloister, and it is natural to suppose
that the mother convent was unwilling to lose a
brother of so ardent a nature and such brilliant theological promise. After some difficulty, probably
caused by differences in the requirements for the
sententiarius as between Wittenberg and Erfurt,[25] he
was received into the theological faculty and en-
trusted in the following months with the responsible
duty of interpreting to the Erfurt students the basic
work of medieval theology, the *Sentences* of Peter
Lombard.[26] The preparatory notes for these lectures
have been preserved as marginal notes in Luther's
handwriting on the edition which he used; they give

---

of Christ as the God of goodness and of grace; and he records this as a capital
point in Luther's theology. This is, however, a long step ahead of Luther's
statements, quoted above, regarding the ideas implanted by Staupitz (cf.
Strohl, *op. cit.*, 120ff., for a discussion of this phase). I need scarcely say that
I do not agree with Strohl in regarding Luther's letter to Staupitz in 1523
and the reference to the general vicar in the letter to the Elector of Saxony
in 1545 as "exaggerations" on Luther's part (cf. *op. cit.*, 116ff.). Luther's
statements, while loosely made, are well supported by other references to the
older counselor, cited above.

[23] Köstlin-Kamrau, *op. cit.*, I, 88.

[24] *Luthers Werdegang*, p. 48.

[25] Cf. letter to the Erfurt faculty, Dec. 21, 1514 (*Enders*, I, 24).

[26] Oergel, *op. cit.*, 115.

the earliest idea of the contents and method of Luther as a lecturer and present valuable evidence as to the stage of religious development which he had reached in 1509. The method followed the hard and fast prescriptions for the work of the theological faculty in the later Middle Ages. The text of the four books of Lombard must be read by the instructor word for word and then interpreted, with an explanation of all difficulties.

It gives one a feeling of deep emotion to turn over the pages of notes which the young lecturer made on the cloister copy of the great medieval dogmatist, now available in the ninth volume of the Weimar edition of Luther's works. We catch something of the enthusiasm—that first great asset of the teacher— with which the young instructor poured new wine into the dry old skins of formalistic medieval dogma. He frankly likes Lombard as one who holds fast the traditions of the Fathers, free from the contaminating findings of human philosophy.[27] Young as he is as teacher, he has evidently worked out a good method of his own, for he seeks to understand thoroughly the background of his subject. To this end he brings to bear all of his training, including the theory of cognition which he had learned from his masters in Erfurt, Trutvetter and Usingen, as well as his mathematics and natural philosophy—all in the manner of one who is sure of his authorities. In the method of the uni-

[27] WA, IX, 29.

versity he attacks the text of his author, and though his occasional comparisons of the various editions of the work are not discursive, but in the form of scattered remarks, we can nevertheless observe an effort to determine the right reading and to make the text explain itself, which is quite in accord with good philological usages and as a method is as valid in the twentieth century as in the days of the Renaissance.

We are able in this work also to see what theological books had provided the basis of his knowledge up to that time. With the retentive memory of the student of the later Middle Ages, he has these at call, and he probably assembled everything within his range of knowledge which might aid in an understanding of the subject. Here, as elsewhere, he appears as a thorough student of a few books rather than as a polyhistorian.

First of all, he knows at first hand something of the writers of his own, the "modernist," school of theology. This includes the commentaries of Occamist direction, Biel's and Peter d'Ailly's. He refers to Hugo of St. Victor's work on the sacrament. He is ready with citations from the Fathers—Dionysius Areopagita, Chrysostom, Jerome, Ambrose, Hilarius —all of whom he may have known in some form of anthology.[28] His reading of Augustine, the most widely read of the Fathers and one enjoying an espe-

[28] In some cases a course in the Fathers preceded at the university the study of Lombard; cf. Neubauer, *Luthers Frühzeit*, 11.

cial authority in Luther's own order, must have begun at a somewhat earlier period,[29] for we have evidence that the great "pillar of the Church," as Luther calls him,[30] was receiving his earnest attention at this time. In a volume of the shorter works of Augustine containing his mystical writings, the work *On the Trinity* and that on *The City of God,* there are marginal annotations in Luther's hand, these notes dating, in the opinion of calligraphists, from approximately the same period as the lectures on Lombard. Of any influence of the Augustinian ideas of grace there is no evidence at this time; indeed Luther declared in the preface of his Latin works in the year before his death that he did not know the anti-Pelagian writings of the great patron of his order, in which the doctrine of grace is especially set forth, until after the discovery of the gospel.[31] The work *On the Spirit and the Letter* he cites very frequently in the Romans lectures six years later.[32]

The young theologian's preparation did not extend merely to the text on which he was lecturing and its grounding in the Fathers. The Bible itself is constantly at hand, and he seeks with such meager equipment as he has to apply to its study the same im-

[29] Lombard cites the African Father more than one thousand times.

[30] *WA,* IX, 23, 12.

[31] *EA, Opp. lat. var. arg.,* I, 23.

[32] That he had at least a superficial knowledge of it at the time of the Lombard lectures is evidenced by a few marginal notes in the volume of Augustine's *Opuscula* (*WA,* IX, 14).

mature but scholarly method which we find elsewhere in the notes. Hebrew and Greek had not been
included in his training, and now he tries slowly but
with determination to open these two gateways to the
first source-book of Christianity. His first knowledge
of Hebrew, as he later writes to his friend Lang,
was obtained from Reuchlin's *Rudimenta*, the first
Hebrew grammar, with glossary attached, published
in Germany. From these he has already learned the
Hebrew letters and their phonetic values.[33] As yet of
course he has no original text of the Bible in Hebrew.
In this and in other ways the notes on Lombard give
evidence that the Humanists had begun to cast their
spell over him, their attraction lying on the philological rather than on the esthetic side. Through
Johann Lang, a fellow-student at the university who
had followed Luther into the convent, there existed
a sort of *liaison* between the Humanists and the
Augustinian cloister in Erfurt, and this cloister friend,
in all probability, furthered Luther's studies in
Greek.[34] These studies are reflected in the Lombard
notes, though there is no reason to suppose that he
was able to get hold of a copy of the Septuagint version of the Bible or a Greek New Testament, or that
Luther's knowledge of the language of the New
Testament was already sufficient for him to use the

[33] *WA*, IX, 63, 28.

[34] Cf. *Briefwechsel von M. Rufus*, 1890, II, 150, Nr. 490; Oergel, *op. cit.*,
17, 133.

original for textual or grammatical observations.[35] Had his knowledge of the two languages of Holy Scriptures been greater than it was, it is yet hardly thinkable that he would have ventured to raise his hands against the canon which made the Vulgate the sacred text. There is no sign that he doubted its absolute and inspired character. The spirit of his lectures is indeed no less scholastic than their subject. In later years Luther recalled that it was Staupitz who impressed on him the importance of becoming a good textual critic, so that he could explain the Bible out of the Bible, yet not neglecting the scholastic sources.

In the Lombard notes the young lecturer shows himself still a faithful adherent of the modernist school. He follows it in his attitude toward philosophy, which he calls the maid-servant *(ancilla)* of theology. Aristotle is "rancid," [36] and a "teller of fables," [37] and it is useless to say that he does not contradict the faith of the Church. The young theologian defends faith and revelation against reason. He bluntly avows himself a modernist and arrays Augustine against Aristotle and the Realists.[38] He still views justification with the eyes of his teachers. His defense of the supernatural standpoint is in their style and already breathes something of the ruthless vigor of the mature Luther: "Never have the fumes

---

[35] Cf. for the *Catholicon* used by Luther, *WA*, IX, 68, 14.

[36] *WA*, IX, 43, 5; 47, 6.   [37] *WA*, IX, 23, 7.   [38] *WA*, IX, 23, 6ff.

of earth lit up the heavens, but have rather hindered light on the earth. I mean that theology is heaven, nay rather the kingdom of the heavens, man and his speculations but smoke. Understand then the reason for so great a diversity of opinion among scholars. Note also that no sow was ever able to teach Minerva, even with all its presumption. Nor have lions and bears been held by spider webs, nor even fish, or birds. Because as a fool I speak foolishly, my boldness and irreverence may merit reproach. For a physical interpretation of theology has even been handed down from holy men and has not been regarded as *lèse majesté*." [39]

In spite of the fact that the theology of the young instructor is to all intents and purposes that which was impressed on him in the lecture rooms of Erfurt and Wittenberg, the marginal notes are marked by a vigorous spirit which indicates a determined and conscientious attempt to ascend to the sources of faith, no matter whither the trail might lead. His deeply tragic conception of sin pictures itself in his references to the struggle which man must wage with "concupiscence," that ever-haunting monster, the ancient fell heritage from Adam. In the longest and most personal passage in the notes [40] he analyzes the nature of sin and compares it to a horse that has broken its rein and is running away with its rider, and he shows the necessity of struggling against it in

[39] *WA*, IX, 65, 12. [40] *WA*, IX, 74-76.

a Latin whose vigor presages the rugged force of the lectures on Romans. His God is still the God of Justice of the scholasts, and His attitude toward the sinner is expressed in the notes with a vividness which reflects Luther's own uneasy soul.

The young teacher is proudly conscious of being orthodox. He still construes grace and free will in the manner of the subtle commentaries of the Occamists; but there is something in the emphasis thrown on the *gift* of grace which is a forerunner of the whirlwind of contempt which he is later going to let loose against the natural will of man. He sums this up in a distich which Denifle ascribes to Albertus Magnus:

Quicquid habes meriti praeventrix gratia donat;
Nil deus in nobis praeter sua dona coronat.[41]
"Whatever thou hast of merit, providing grace endows;
Naught doth God crown in us save gifts which He bestows."

Also in the spirit with which he defends grace there is something of the coming battle-cry against the schoolmen, that they have despised Holy Scripture: [42] "What nature is not able to comprehend, may be attained by the truth of Scriptures and of faith."

[41] *WA*, IX, 72, 27; Luther quotes it again in his sermon on Tauler (*WA*, IX, 99).

[42] *WA*, IX, 45, 6.

The framework of the marginal notes on Lombard is then the ancient and traditional structure, but there is growing within this frame a spirit of trust in the grace of God and a reliance on Holy Scriptures which shows that the soul struggles of the young monk had not been in vain. Modern critics have found the tone of the Lombard notes vain and disputatious.[43] After more than four centuries they still breathe forth something of the vigorous spirit of youth seeking to adapt itself to tradition and authority, yet at the same time holding in leash a powerful, explosive force.

The lectures on the *Sentences* may have been concluded in the late summer or early fall of 1510. The sources do not permit us to follow in detail the events of the following two years nor determine the exact relation of Luther to the cloister and its studies. It may be assumed, however, that at least during a part of that time he gave lectures on the Bible and perhaps acted as a sub-regent of theological studies in the Augustinian cloister. For the summer of 1512 we find him under orders of his superior Staupitz preparing to take the doctor's degree. The intervening period included a chapter in his life to which he afterwards attached the greatest importance, the journey to Rome.

"I would not take," Luther declared more than a quarter of a century later, "one thousand florins for

[43] Grisar, *op. cit.*, I, 47.

having seen and heard Rome." [44] The dramatic
figure presented by the presence of the future antag-
onist of the Roman Church in the citadel of ecclesiastical powers and abuses has stimulated an immense
amount of research, although there are no contemporary sources of primary value, and our knowledge
of the purposes and circumstances of the memorable
journey depends on recollections of the aging
Luther, recollections which are tinged for the most
part by polemical considerations, and on such col-
lateral evidence as tireless investigators have brought
together. Built up on this evidence is the hypothesis
which ascribes the journey of Luther to Rome to the
agitation within the order of the Augustine Eremites
on account of the proposed extension by Staupitz of
the strict observance to other cloisters of the order.
The question was undoubtedly of influence on the
religious development of Luther, and it would be
interesting to know how far the opposition of the
Erfurt and certain other reformed cloisters to the
union of the Saxon unreformed cloisters with the
reformed stimulated Luther's own ascetic observances.

Of the facts of the Roman journey our only knowledge is derived from scattered remarks of Luther in
sermons and *Table Talk* many years later, at a time
when Rome and all its associations had been colored
by the great struggle over indulgences. But even

[44] *TR*, V, 5484; cf. *TR*, III, 3582A-1537.

though viewed through strongly colored glasses of prejudice, Luther's reminiscences contain much that was characteristic of the young monk and indicative of his development. "I ran," he declares afterwards, "through all the churches and crypts of the city like a crazy saint." It is significant that none of the impressions of the Roman journey which remained was artistic. Michelangelo was then at work on the ceiling of the Sistine Chapel and Raphael on the walls of the Vatican Stanze; the frescoes of Pinturicchio were then as now open to view and the dome of St. Peter's was rising, but no recollections regarding these remained in Luther's mind, or at least none was fresh enough to find place in his memoirs. The ancient monuments served only to point the tale of God's just judgments on the weakness of man. The Pantheon remains in his sermons to the end of his life as a reminder of Christ's victory over the gods of heathendom. He had no eyes for the great paintings of the Renaissance, but recalled a picture in the cloister where he lodged painted by St. Luke himself.[45] With burning heart he descended into the catacombs and he revels in fantastic figures in later years when speaking of martyrs buried there.[46] "I believed everything that was invented with lies and stinks!"[47] Among other marvels he saw the twelve-foot rope

[45] WA, XLVII, 817-1539.

[46] Unterricht auf etliche Artikel, WA, II, 72; TR, II, 2709b, III, 3479a; V, 6447; 6463; EA, XXX, 192.

[47] WA, XXXI, 1, 226.

with which Judas hanged himself. He heard and said innumerable masses.[48] "I, like a fool," he declares, "carried onions to Rome and brought back garlic." [49] In spite of all of his piety, he could not have been more blind than his contemporaries to the abuses in Rome, which had been pictured as a "foul sewer of all crimes" since the days of Savonarola; and his recollections teem with references to cloisters and churches which had been devoured by popes and cardinals as well as to the libertinism of certain cardinals. As to Michelangelo, Rome becomes to him within a few years and remains throughout life "mother and nurse of all sins."

When Luther returned from the center and heart of the Church, he was no doubt disillusioned and to some extent disheartened by what he had seen and heard. Nevertheless the fabric of faith in his heart was not as yet weakened thereby. Far more of error clung to the Church than he had believed. Sin walked in the highest places. The dispute within the cloisters over observance plays scarcely any rôle in his letters and memories; but it may well have been of cardinal significance in his life. It may have given him opportunity to deepen the impression of his ability as a scholar and his force as a man on Staupitz and the convents at Wittenberg and Erfurt; for in September, 1512, the brothers, assembled in convoca-

---

[48] WA, XXXVIII, 211; TR, III, 3428; cf. TR, V, 5484-1542.
[49] WA, XLVII, 392.

tion at Cologne, gave evidence of a confidence in him in both capacities. The chapter elected him sub-prior of the Wittenberg cloister and directed him to apply for the degree of doctor of theology so that he might take up the Biblical professorship which Staupitz held.

VI

THE LECTURES ON PSALMS

THE young monk and priest had become a teacher of theology. The monk who had for five years battled with the haunting specter of sin unforgiven, of grace not fully attained, with the terrors of predestination, was now to guide younger men into an understanding of the nature of sin and grace. The young theological student who had set out to find a formula which should combine a Nominalistic understanding of repentance and grace with conceptions drawn from Gerson and others and perhaps fortified by suggestions from Staupitz, that God leads to repentance and grace through despair in ourselves,[1] must now bring this formula before his students. The necessity for teaching was undoubtedly of importance in clarifying Luther's mind and in developing independence of thought. The difficulty is no longer merely a personal one, but a struggle to reach firm ground from which he might guide others, an examination of the sources to find comfort and constructive ideas for those seekers placed between hope and fear, as he had been a few years earlier.

[1] Strohl, *op. cit.*, I, 108.

As the marginal notes on Lombard show, he was beginning to make breaches in the wall of Occamist intellectualism which his teachers had built around his thinking. Already he had found his way through Lombard directly to Augustine, the great teacher whom Lombard constantly quotes and whom Luther is shortly to make one of the pillars of his own system. Gerson, Bonaventure, William of Paris and others have fed him with comfort. While as yet Luther has not felt the full force of Augustine's drive against the possibility of man's coöperation in winning God's grace, as he is soon to do in the African Father's anti-Pelagian writings, nevertheless his own consciousness of the reality of sin has been powerfully enforced by the tremendous realism with which Augustine places the sinner before an angered God. Martin has also undoubtedly felt something of the powerful reality of the love of God as it appears in the works of the great patron of his order. Even if, as seems likely, the discovery that the justice of God (*iustitia Dei*) is none other than the mercy of God (*gratia Dei*) has not yet dawned upon him, the mind of the young theologian already foreshadowed a more direct idea of God's forgiveness than that set forth in the metaphysical refinements of his scholastic teachers.

Just when the final transfer from Erfurt to Wittenberg came, we do not know. It is probable that Luther shared the "exile" which we know fell upon his friend Johann Lang for differing with the general vicar Staupitz and the resisting observant cloisters.[2] A hostile contemporary of Luther's, Cochlaeus,[3] claimed to have heard from Erfurt monks of Luther's "falling away to Staupitz." At any rate, the return to the Wittenberg cloister and university offered a field less hedged about with tradition than the scene of his first steps in the religious life. He may have gone to Wittenberg in the fall of 1511; in any event he was there early in the following May,[4] and possibly represented the Wittenberg Augustinians at the chapter meeting held in Cologne in May,[5] which elevated him to be sub-prior of the small convent at Wittenberg.[6]

Before this he had in all probability overcome his hesitation in taking the professorship in Bible, coupled with the additional duty of preaching. It is clear that his mind was still in turmoil regarding cardinal points in theology when we read that he resisted these responsibilities to the point of offense against authority.[7] Twenty years later he recalled the spot in the cloister court at Wittenberg where Staupitz had laid the duties of preaching and Bible teaching upon him and he had urged fifteen reasons against them, to no purpose.[8] One of these reasons was that

[2] Usingen, quoted by Oergel; cf. Böhmer, *Luthers Romfahrt*, 61.

[3] *Paraclesin*, 1524, Bll. C 2, quoted by Scheel, II, 428, Anm. 16.

[4] Cf. letter to Eberbach, May 8, 1512 (Oergel, *op. cit.*, 133).

[5] *WA*, XXXIV, 1, 22.

[6] Kolde, *Augustiner Congregation*, 243; cf. *TR*, I, 241-1532.

[7] Letter of Dec. 21, 1514 (*Enders*, I, 24).

[8] Cf. *TR*, II, 2255a-1531; V, 5371-1540.

he was a sick man and had not long to live, but the intense labor which he underwent in the following years makes it certain that the difficulty lay not in his physical health, but in the dread which he felt on thinking over the responsibilities of the Biblical chair and of explaining the Word from the pulpit, in view of the fact that he was not sure that he had himself fulfilled all the demands of a just God.

He had not indeed met even the minimum requirements for the doctorate in theology, a degree of surpassing honor and responsibility. Erfurt required ten years as a minimum, and the records of the theological faculty there produce cases where eighteen years were devoted to the study of theology before the degree was granted.[9] To admit him, even the less exacting requirement of Wittenberg had to be waived by the discriminatory power of the faculty. Thus, "forced by Staupitz," Luther ascended to the highest grade of theological study.[10] The event was celebrated with all the pomp and circumstance which the university was capable of displaying, accompanied by a field-day for the performances of the champions of medieval dialectics. The young candidate swore solemn oaths of obedience to Church and university, and received, first the license to preach, and then the open and closed Bible and the golden doctor-ring of theology. Within a year he had begun his lectures as professor of Bible, lectures which were in less than

[9] Oergel, op. cit., 96.   [10] TR, IV, 4091-1538; cf. II, 2739.

five years to break completely through the shell of scholastic theology and lead the lecturer from academic halls into the arena of world politics.

This is a period of continual inward development which cannot be traced in all of its steps. As has been remarked already, even were the sources at our command far more abundant than they are, the mysteries of personality are too profound for penetration, and the influences which played their stately music on the chords of his soul too complex for us to be able to do more than seek a few of the major ones. Like most men of powerful will, Luther regarded his life in restrospect as a series of crises, and at each of these he felt that God had thrown a brilliant light on his pathway. What to the student at this distance appears as a gradual shaking off of scholastic tradition and a gradual widening of the horizon was to him a series of more than natural experiences, each a milestone on the long road toward the true understanding of justification.

Such a crisis was that which Protestant tradition has designated "the discovery of the gospel." Viewed in retrospect from Luther's old age, it takes its place beside the experience of the forest of Stotternheim which preceded his entry into the cloister as surrounded by an atmosphere of the sudden and miraculous. The importance which he later attaches to the experience cannot be denied. He refers to it in every decade of his subsequent life. "I felt myself re-born and entering into the open gates of Paradise itself," he declares in summing up his religious experience in the oft-quoted preface written in the year before his death.[11] The importance which he assigns to it and the suddenness surrounding the experience are reflected in many passages from the recollections of friends who heard his conversations on the subject and from students who heard his lectures.[12] Nearly twenty years later Luther recalled in a conversation, if the testimony of two members of his household group may be trusted (Cordatus and Lauterbach), the exact place where the gospel light burst upon him—the tower of the Gray Cloister in Wittenberg and in all probability his study room there.[13]

The importance which Luther assigns to the event makes it necessary for us to examine as closely as possible the character of this sudden inspiration. In the passage written in 1545, so often referred to, in speaking of the year 1519 and the exegetical labors which preceded it, he declares that he had burned with the ardent wish to understand a term employed in the first chapter of the Epistle to the Romans, in

[11] *EA, Opp. lat. var. arg.,* I, 23.

[12] Scheel, *Dokumente zu Luthers Entwickelung,* 15, 20, 23, 39, 48, 49, 69; Müller, *Luthers Werdegang,* 118.

[13] *TR,* III, 3232ab-1532; cf. 3874-1538; *TR,* II, 1681-1532. Cf. regarding the dispute about the meaning of *"hypocaustum,"* a term which Luther elsewhere applies to his workroom, *Enders,* VI, 117; *de Wette,* V, 791; cf. Grisar, *op. cit.,* I, 323; Scheel, *Luther,* II, 435, Anm. 13; Boehmer's note, *op. cit.,* 3 Aufl., p. 39; also a suggestion of Strohl, *L'évolution réligieuse de Luther,* 142, Anm. 3.

which it is said that the "justice of God is revealed in the gospel," and had up to that time thought of it with trembling. "Finally God took pity upon me. While I was meditating day and night and examining the connection of these words, 'That the justice of God is revealed in the gospel, as it is written, the just man lives by faith, I commenced to understand that the justice of God means here that justice by which the righteous man lives through the gift of God, that is to say, through faith.[14] The sense of the phrase is then this: The gospel reveals to us the justice of God, but the *passive* justice of God by which God in his mercy justifies us by means of faith—the just man shall live by faith."

Here again it seems undeniable that, in accordance with the psychology of the time and his own ardent temperament, Luther clothed in the form of an illuminating vision that which the subtle workings of his own mind absorbed through years of anxious speculation on the problem of human sin and divine justice. The text to which he refers, Romans i.,17, had already caused him thought when he was preparing his lectures on Peter Lombard in the Erfurt cloister. Indeed, both in his soul experiences and his studies the subject must have hung in the background during many hours of cloister meditation. Behind grace and the justification through grace there loomed

---

[14] "*Ibi iustitia dei coepi intelligere eam, qua iustus dono dei vivit, nempe ex fide.*"

always a God of punishment. Ever and anew evil desire *(concupiscentia)*, he tells us in a sermon of 1514-15,[15] brought guilt upon him in the sight of his conscience, so that he was almost obliged to despair. He could not appear before God decorated with merit, he writes to his friend Spalatin about the same time.[16] There stood constantly before him the "justice of God," which in spite of his life in accordance with the monastic rule made him tremble as a sinner before God, for he had no certainty that God was appeased by his penance. This "justice" he had always interpreted as the justice which rewards and punishes; and he felt with trembling that such justice must stamp him as guilty. Looking back upon this period in after years, he says, "I hurled myself upon this term *(vocabulum illud)*, the 'justice of God,' which I explained according to custom thus: The justice of God is the quality which makes of Him a God who is just and who punishes sinners. It is thus that all the doctors had interpreted this passage with the exception of Saint Augustine: 'The justice of God is the wrath of God'." [17] Now a new light broke upon him, and in proportion as he had previously hated the term "justice of God" he now cherished "the very sweet word" *(dulcissimum vocabulum)*, for God's justice began to appear to him as the justice by which a merciful God makes us just through faith.

[15] *WA*, IV, 665; cf. *Ficker*, I, 2, 102.   [16] April 8, 1516 (*Enders*, I, 29).
[17] *Enarr. in Gen.*, Cap. XXVII, 38 (*WA*, XLIII, 537).

It has been abundantly shown by Denifle and others, and would now doubtless be admitted by even the most ardent of Luther apologists, that this discovery was in no sense a discovery for theological scholarship of the Middle Ages, and that what the young professor saw in a brilliant flash of inspiration many inspired scholars of the Church had felt and seen before him.[18] Hirsch [19] has demonstrated, however, that Luther's master Biel, whose definitions Luther knew by heart, had interpreted the term *iustitia dei* in the active, judicial sense. In accepting the passage from the lectures on Genesis from which Luther's remark was taken, we encounter the same possibility of error as attaches to other passages in Luther's works which depend on the notebooks of students as their source. Before the experience had assumed the cardinal significance in his mind which it attained in retrospect, Luther himself admits that the theologians may have interpreted Paul's words in this way *theoretically*, but that they certainly did not practice their interpretation. Furthermore, Luther was no expert in church history, and although the discovery may have been no discovery for the theological world, it certainly was one for him. We find him in the last years of his life still firm in the belief that neither Augustine nor any one else had preceded

[18] Denifle, *Luther*, I, 2, 537ff., holds that not a single Catholic writer had understood the passage in the sense to which Luther objects; cf. Boehme, *Luther im Lichte d. neueren Forschung*, 3. Aufl., 69ff.

[19] *Initium theologiae Lutheri*, 150ff.

him in a clear understanding of Paul's phrase and in its application to life.[20] There is every evidence that it represented a soul experience that gave him a vitally new assurance in his inner religious life and in his administration of his office as teacher and religious leader. Very soon thereafter and henceforth he proclaims Paul the most profound of theologians.[21]

Just when the new flash of intelligence came and this new assurance began to develop in his life, it is as impossible to say as it is to trace the subtle working of the spirit in the hidden laboratory of the subconscious mind. Protestant theologians of Germany and France in the past two decades, who yield nothing in acuteness of vision nor dialectical subtlety in comparison with the contemporaries of Thomas Aquinas or Duns Scotus, have sought eagerly to locate with definiteness the moment of this awakening. To call the names of those who have attempted to localize Luther's discovery in point of time would be to pass in review practically all the leading Protestant students of Luther and all the savants in the field of religious dogma in the past twenty years. O. Ritschl[22] and Seeberg[23] set the discovery of the buried truth as early as the Erfurt lectureship. Scheel[24] would put it in the period of the preparation

[20] *EA, Opp. lat. var arg.*, I, 23; *Enarr. in Gen.* (*WA*, XLIII, 537-1541-42).
[21] *WA*, III, 31.
[22] *Dogmengeschichte d. protest. Theologie*, 2. Aufl., 1912, 9.
[23] *Op. cit.*, 69ff.
[24] *Luther*, II, 437, Anm. 17.

of the lectures on Psalms, in the summer of 1513. Boehmer [25] inclines now to the same opinion; while Müller locates the discovery as late as the end of 1514.

The light on the *terminus ad quem* which we should expect to find in Luther's use of the *iustitia Dei* in the lectures on Psalms, probably commenced in the midsummer of 1513, is obscured by a series of philological difficulties. The lecturer interprets the *iustitia Dei* in the new sense in the lecture on the first Psalm, but not again in this manner until the second part of the work (after page 35 of the *WA*). It has been suggested [26] that this was due to a reëditing of this portion by Luther, but H. Thomas [27] has studied the manuscript and finds no trace of such reëditing. Various suggestions have been made in explanation, none altogether satisfactory.[28] The keenest eyes of German and French savants have been directed toward finding traces of the new understanding in the Lombard notes.[29] The subtle hypotheses which

---

[25] 3. Aufl. 52.

[26] Hirsch, *op. cit.*, 161-165.

[27] *Zur Würdigung der Psalmenvorlesungen Luthers*, 1920.

[28] Müller, *Werdegang*, etc., 128 ff. suggests a replacement of the earlier pages of the original manuscript by a later version of Luther's.

[29] Cf. for a review of possible hints of the new idea in the marginal notes on the *Sentences*, Strohl, II, 145 ff. Attention has been called here to what is possibly a new conception of faith and it is asserted that the "acquired faith" (*fides aquisita*) Luther already regards as the faith which saves by taking hold of the Saving Christ (cf. *WA*, IX, 17, 39, 43). Others find that Luther's assertion in the marginal notes that the three theological virtues—faith, hope and love—are contemporaneous, a view widely held among the Augustinians, opens the way directly from faith to good works, for such an

have resulted, resting in the main on very fine shades of distinction and in part ascribing to Luther a dialectical refinement not shown elsewhere in his theological thinking, do little more than raise the probability that he had already in 1509 some elementary ideas of justifying faith as he later conceived of it. His emphasis in the marginal notes on Christ as our faith and our justice; his self-condemnation under the judgment of conscience without despair, indicate that he had at that time an inkling of the saving way without being able to think it through to clarity. He was seeking the light and hope had begun to break through, though as yet pale on the horizon.

It cannot be overlooked that Luther's reference to the cloister tower at Wittenberg or that of his reporters, is of a piece with his constant tendency to dramatize the stages of his religious development, and the "discovery" can at most represent only one step in his progress toward assurance of soul. Nevertheless the sources show a marked development in his attitude toward grace and penance in the four years between the marginal notes made in Erfurt on Peter Lombard's *Sentences* and the first lectures on Psalms. A quarter of a century later he recalls that the salvation of the

integration between the theological virtues and good actions would do away with the *fides informis*, lying according to scholastic authority between the *fides aquisita* and *fides formata* (cf. Müller, *Theol. Quellen*, 182ff; *Werdegang*, 106ff.) Luther would thus make justifying faith a direct and gratuitous gift of God, a revolutionary innovation as compared with the Occamist school of theology.

gospel was not known to him until after he became a doctor, [30] and he says in another sermon at the same time that he even sought to obtain the justice of God through the merit of the saints.[31] Whereas on the one hand the Erfurt lecturer still presents to his hearers the grace that makes men pleasant to God *(gratia gratiam faciens)* and the love which has its roots in worthiness before God, on the other hand in his first lecture on Psalms he charges the theologians of his day with being ignorant of the great truth of St. Paul which had been buried and which he had dug up.[32]

The revolution must have been like other stages in soul development, the result of years of reflection. The interpretation of Paul's words, which he later recalled as having come to him in a flash, appears even in such sources as we possess to have ripened through a period of years, a period which began with the intense study of Augustine in preparing the marginal notes for the Lombard lectures in Erfurt, developed as necessity arose for working out the exegetical explanation of Psalms in 1513, and gained in significance as the young professor wrote out his lectures on the Epistle to the Romans and warmed to the struggle over indulgences. He states quite categorically in the last year of his life that, after the true meaning of the "justice of God" had been revealed to him, he reviewed in memory the texts where this phrase

[30] *WA*, XLV, 86-1537.   [31] *EA*, XLVI, 78-1537.   [32] *WA*, III, 31.

occurs and sought for other terms which it was necessary to explain in the same fashion; that he read Augustine's *On the Letter and the Spirit* and was surprised to find that he too interpreted the "justice of God" in a passive fashion, that is, the justice with which God clothes us when he justifies us. This narrative of his development has then brought him to the beginning of his second course in Psalms, in other words to the year 1519.[33] The beginning of the first course on Psalms lies then nearly midway between his first attempts at interpreting in lectures the dogmatic basis of Christian faith and the year which he sets as the final stage of his development. It thus becomes the axis, as it were, of a decade of search for an interpretation of the way in which God saves man.

It is an inspiring thought, and one which no academically trained person can overlook, that this critical point in Luther's development, so significant for the religious and political history of Europe in the centuries that followed, really developed out of an academic and in its essence a theological problem, the problem of understanding and ultimately presenting to his students how the *iustitia Dei* is revealed in the gospel. No clearer proof could be offered that the

[33] Scheel has assumed that Luther's reference to 1519 is due to a lapse of memory and that he really had in mind the *first* course of lectures on Psalms, but this explanation does violence to the sources. In his review of his theological development Luther begins with the second course of lectures on Psalms as a starting point in his narrative, retraces the course of his thought in the preceding period and then returns to the starting point.

real mainsprings of history are not materialistic impulses but transcendental ideas. The Reformation with all of its wide implications did not spring from social, political or economic causes. Its origin lay in the fact that a monk-professor, out of the depths of a rich soul experience, finally interpreted a theological concept, *iustitia Dei,* not in the sense of the justice which condemns *(iustitia damnans),* as his master Biel had done, but as the mercy which saves *(misericordia salvans).*[34]

The first duty demanded of the young doctor of theology was to teach, and the burden of Biblical lectures fell heavily upon him immediately after he had received his degree. The Wittenberg school of theology demanded the interpretation of the Psalms and the Epistles, and he now flung himself with ardor into a task upon which he had entered with many misgivings. Although our knowledge of Luther's lecture courses during this period is not without its obscure spots, enough is known to enable us to follow the young scholar's career as teacher with some exactness. In a period of about six and one-half years he seems to have given seven lecture courses. All of these, with the exception of the course on the Epistle to Titus, have come down to us, in part in the original manuscripts of Luther's notes, in part in the transcripts of the students of theology who sat on the benches before him. On October 18, 1512, he re-

[34] Cf. Hirsch, *op. cit.,* Anm. 2.

ceived his degree, and in the middle of July of the following year he opened his first course of lectures, that on the Psalms. This he continued until March, 1515. Before he brought this course to a conclusion he must have already been hard at work on the course on the Epistle to the Romans, which began perhaps in the spring of that year and continued until the summer of 1516.[35] It is possible that this was followed by the course on Titus. On October 27, 1516, he began the course on the Epistle to the Galatians, which he then continued through the winter semester; and finally toward the end of 1518 he began to deliver his second course on Psalms. Somewhere within these years, possibly in 1517-18, came the lectures on the Epistle to the Hebrews.[36] The course of lectures on Psalms in 1513-15 and those on Romans 1515-16 occupy a critical position in his religious development and must therefore be examined with great care.

In both courses the lecturer followed the medieval system which he had learned at Erfurt, and from which he deviated little during the thirty years of his Biblical professorship. Indeed, if one may trust expressions in the *Table Talk*,[37] he took no little pride in later years in his command of the dialectical method so dear to those trained in scholastic philosophy. Apparently all of the lectures were written out

[35] *Ficker*, 1, XLVI.
[36] Chronology from Boehmer, *Luthers Romfahrt*, 15.
[37] *TR*, I, 193; II, 2629a,b.

with great precision and delivered from notes according to the scholastic technique, which demanded that the text be first read to the students, then analyzed and explained.[38] The respect which such a method presupposed for the *word* was absolute, and for the treatment of the Divine Word in its presentation to students preliminary precautions were taken that involved an amount of labor which the modern professor would find truly appalling.

For the first course on Psalms we have two manuscripts, both in the hand of Luther himself and approaching the subject from different angles. The first is a copy of the Latin Vulgate text of the Psalms which the young professor had the Wittenberg printer Gruneberg prepare, using for that purpose one of the many editions of the Latin Bible then available.[39] On this text Luther made an interlinear and marginal glossary, the former explaining individual words and the latter establishing the connection with illustrative citations, religious and ethical comments, and contemporary references of various kinds. Accompanying this textual apparatus or *glossae,* we have in the other manuscript, in accordance with medieval custom, the *scholia,* also in Luther's handwriting. In these the lecturer discusses freely the basic thoughts of the work, and debates with his predecessors and

[38] The title of the Dresden Ms., *Dictata super psalterium,* indicates the method; cf. *WA*, III, Kawerau's introduction, 7ff.

[39] Ficker counts nineteen of these which appeared in the years 1509-1516; cf. *Ficker,* 1, XLVII.

opponents, drawing on a wide range of authors, as well as contemporary history, for illustration and support.

In addition we have, also in Luther's hand, a series of marginal notes, *Adnotationes,* on the leaves of an edition of the Psalms in French and Latin [40] by the French humanist Lefèvre d'Étaples (Faber Stapulensis), printed in Paris in 1509. Here, according to a method which we have seen that he had practiced four years earlier with the *Sentences* of Lombard, Luther wrote down his own ideas on the Psalms quite freely. In the formation of these ideas the French exegist undoubtedly played an important rôle. Luther mentions him repeatedly in the lectures themselves. He thus uses the text of Faber Stapulensis to note down ideas on the Psalms which were afterwards to be used in the preparation of material for dictation to his students.[41]

When the young professor faced his group of theological students for his first course of lectures, either in July or, more probably, at the beginning of the

[40] *Quincuplex psalterium Gallicum, Romanum Hebraicum Vetus Conciliatum;* cf. *WA,* IV, 463 ff.

[41] Kawerau (*WA,* IV, 465) assumes that Luther prepared the *Adnotationes* first, following these with the *glossae* and the *scholia* but Hedwig Thomas, *Zur Würdigung von Luthers Psalmenvorlesung,* 51, concludes on the basis of an investigation of Luther's shifting attitude, with its mixture of old and new interpretations, that no one of the three—*adnotationes, glossae* or *scholia* —as we now have them shows a logical development of Luther's thought. The conclusion is that additions, intercalations and retouchings are to be found in all.

winter semester in October 1513, [42] he looked back
upon a year of intensive preparation. The interpretation of the Psalms, the longest single work in the
Bible, called for an immense output of energy:
glossae and *scholia* in the Weimar edition comprise
over one hundred folio pages of print. In its self-
contradictory attitude toward the fundamental idea
of God's justice, the work shows that the labor of
study and readjustment went on in all likelihood
through the entire two years which the lectures took
in delivery. From the first pages there is evidence
of an intense study of previous exegists, a whole
galaxy of whom appears, from St. Augustine and Cas-
siodorus to such recent writers as Nicholas of Lyra
and Paul of Burgos. Interesting is the glimpse which
the book gives into the soul of the young teacher, as
he stands still dependent on these sources and yet
struggling to reach an independent view of the
Biblical text. Intriguing is the problem of finding
in his monastic Latin, where the thought is still
strait-jacketed into the rigid forms of scholastic
exegesis, the evidence of the dawn of a new light.
The conception of God's relation to man through
grace which he builds up on Augustine's mystical
thought is often tangled and obscure. The controversial bent of Occam's school of theology shows itself
constantly, and the thread of thought loses itself again
and again in an intricate and sheerly interminable web

[42] Cf. H. Thomas, *op. cit.*, 50.

of philosophical, ethical and theological ideas.[43] Like Michelangelo's slave, the young scholar seeks to wind himself free from the unyielding stone of scholastic systems. Modern scholars have sought to dissect out of a series of disconnected and sometimes self-contradictory elements in the long, long commentary the Neo-Platonism of Augustine and the African Father's conception of sin and grace, and the theological concepts and the mysticism of St. Bernard.[44]

The theology of the young teacher is still plainly in the making. It is, however, not hard to see that in the two years and more during which the lectures were prepared and delivered Luther was not merely spinning a web out of the hair-drawn wires of dialectics, but was engaged in a personal soul struggle, the stakes of which were ultimate peace of mind regarding the paramount question of religious life. Throughout the tangled, disconnected and often obscure notes there glows always the fear of sin and its awful consequences for him who does not possess the grace of God. Behind it all looms again and again the great prepossession of the tender medieval conscience, the fear of sudden death. Unsolved is the old problem which thrusts itself more and more into the foreground as the study of Augustine increasingly absorbs his attention—the futility of human effort in

[43] Cf. Grisar, *op. cit.*, I, 59.

[44] Hunzinger, *Luther und die deutsche Mystik*, 97.

the face of the awful question of predestination.[45]
Ever present is the gnawing sense of sin for which the
sacrament seems to bring him no peace.

If we see the struggles, we also see, however, the
breaking through of a new light. Through the
meshes of scholastic controversial argument we see
him gradually adopting and adapting Augustine's
argument. For here, as in the notes on Peter Lombard, it is Augustine who attracts him, and the
African Father now exceeds by far in importance all
other authorities. Here at last is a vibrant soul loving
piety that forms a great contrast to the dry scholasts
with their differentiations and dissections of grace.
Here is a man with realistic ideas of sin like his own.
So often does Luther transcribe the thoughts of
Augustine that an effort has been made to show that
he had completely absorbed the Neo-Platonism of the
great patron of his order and that under the influence
of these ideas he had for the time at least turned his
back on the Nominalism of his Erfurt preceptors and
of his great master Biel.[46] To accept such a theory
would be to ascribe to Luther a comprehension of
philosophy and habit of abstract thought which he
did not have at the time of the Psalms lectures or at
any other time. As has been pointed out above, his
method of developing thought was impulsive and
naïve rather than reflective and abstract. He found

[45] Braun, op. cit., 18ff; WA, IV, 227ff.
[46] Cf. Hunzinger, op. cit., 4 and passim.

in the mystical writings of Augustine, in the *Soliloquies, Concerning Real Religion* and the *Confessions,* an exhilarating spirit of piety and a lyrical eloquence in presenting the transcendent charms of the love-life of the spirit, and he was intoxicated with it. He repeats these words of the African Father in his lectures, hoping that his students will respond to the same thrill at the beauty of the piety expressed in them as he had. It is hardly likely that he appreciated their philosophical bearing or was at all aware that they contained epistemological ideas that were in conflict with those of his philosophical masters.[47] What he found in Augustine and quoted from him were the rapturous and beautiful passages which glorify the invisible and sing the phrases of the transcendent realities of the life of the spirit.[48]

Influenced beyond doubt by the mystic atmosphere of Augustine's ideas is the attitude of the lecturer toward grace as shown by his interpretation of the *iustitia Dei.* Fascinating is the problem of seeking to find in the long discussions in the *scholia* a shift of theological position so big with importance for Luther's future conception of grace. Several German scholars, notably Loofs,[49] Hirsch,[50] and Loofs' scholar Hedwig Thomas,[51] have sought to do this, in-

---

[47] Cf. Strohl, *op. cit.,* II, 167ff; Scheel, *Luther,* II, 235 and notes. Both take issue with Hunzinger on this point.

[48] Cf. Hunzinger, *op. cit.,* 41-45.   [49] *Theolog. Stud. Krit.,* 1917, 328ff.

[50] "*Initium theolog. Luth.,*" *Theolog. Stud. Krit.,* 1920, 153-169.

[51] *Zur Würdigung,* etc.

duced perhaps by Luther's statement in the autobiographical sketch often referred to connecting the primal fact of his soul life, his new understanding of the "justice of God," with the lectures on Psalms, and stating that he did not enjoy the Psalter until he understood correctly the *iustitia Dei*.[52]

Luther occupies himself again and again with the conception of the *iustitia Dei* in the early course of lectures on Psalms, showing that it was one of the ideas that now obsessed him. The doctrine that he had acquired from his teachers was that God crowns only the merits acquired under the stimulus and with the aid of his grace. Man must become just in order that God may accept him. In discussing four of the Psalms (x, xviii, lxxix, cxxi) we find this idea set forth. The relation of man to God appears as a *legal* relation, and man may only find acceptance with God through the justice of the law. The *iustitia Dei* is therefore an active justice *(iustitia dei activa)*.[53] This culminates in the statement that no one is just except the one who is obedient.[54] God is actively *(intrinsice)* just, and before him man can exist only through his own active justice and holiness. In this interpretation which Luther found in the exegists and other scholars whom he follows, re-

[52] He refers here to the second course of lectures of 1519; but as has been pointed out he is speaking undoubtedly of his entire course of development during the period of his early lectures.

[53] Cf. Thomas, *op. cit.*, 15 ff.

[54] *"Nullus est justus nisi obediens"* (*WA*, IV, 405, 24).

mission and justification are separated by the necessity for the infusion of grace,[55] and this infusion
comes to us through the sacrament. In addition to
this traditional theory which he took over from his
teachers, we find another interpretation when the
young scholar comes to discuss in long *scholia* Psalms
i and l. Here the lecturer seeks consolation in the
fact that salvation is *unconditional.* How then does
justification come to man? By condemning himself
and affirming that he is a sinner, for by this means he
justifies God, since he says of himself what God says
of him.[56] The beginning of this justification is that
the sinner accuses himself.[57] So he declares, "The
justice of God will not arise within us unless first
of all our own justice falls and perishes."

This necessary adjustment of self becomes one of
Luther's favorite formulas through the years immediately following. We note it in a letter to Spalatin
in 1518.[58] Stressed heavily in Psalms, it occurs less
often in the Romans lectures and less and less in later
works.[59] "This doctrine," he declares, "of the most
profound theologian Paul is unknown to our theologians to-day, whether speculatively I know not,
but practically I know." [60]

[55] *"Infusio gratiae"*; cf. Loofs, *op. cit.,* 346.

[56] *WA*, III, 289, 32ff.

[57] *"Iustus enim in principio est accusator sui"* (*WA*, III, 29, 16).

[58] Feb. 15 (*Enders*, I, 154).   [59] Loofs, *op. cit.,* 415.

[60] *"Haec est disputatio profundissimi theologi Pauli Apostoli nostris hodie theologis, an speculative nescio, practice scio quod ignotissima"* (*WA*, III, 31, 14ff).

This then is the *iustitia passiva* to which Luther refers in later life, the justice with which God makes just.[61] It commences and continues with accusation of self. Man remains always just and always a sinner. What a new light must have burst upon him when he caught this idea and the corollary to it, that the essence of God consists in his communicating his justice to those who have no right to it! "This is the essence of God: not to receive good things, but to give them." [62] No wonder that in retrospect it seemed to him that the gates of Paradise had opened before him, for what now appeared to him was not a God of vengeance but a living God of grace. Hereafter he fixed his eyes on what was soon to become for him the "article by which the church must stand or fall." [63] For here lies in elementary form and struggling for expression the great dogma which was later to become the mainspring of his whole religious system—justification by faith. Repeatedly in the Psalms lectures he identifies *justificatio* and *fides*.[64] The faith which recognizes our own unworthiness and the necessity for Christ's redemption and believes

[61] Not until 1531 is the term *iustitia passiva* employed; cf. Hirsch, *op. cit.*, 157. Here Luther justifies his interpretation grammatically in a discussion in his Genesis commentary (*EA, Ex. opp. lat.*, X, 154-157). The same idea is contained in the Psalms lectures (*WA*, III, 458, 8ff; cf. Loofs, *op. cit.*, 353).

[62] "*Hoc est esse Deum: non accipere bona, sed dare*" (*WA*, IV, 269, 25).

[63] "*Articulus stantis et cadentis ecclesiae.*"

[64] "*Iustitiam tuam fidei*" (*WA*, III, 200, 18); "*in iustitia tua, quae est ex fide*" (*WA*, III, 66, 6); "*iustitia, . . . quae est sola fides*" (III, 320, 20); "*quod iustitia est credere deo*" (*WA*, III, 331, 3).

that God wishes our salvation brings about an understanding between the soul and God which is justification. The justification of the Christian becomes synonymous with Faith. Faith justifies.[65] Two years later in the lectures on Romans the young teacher clarifies the idea in an early scholion: "Justification passive and active and faith or belief in Him are the same. Because we justify his words, the gift of himself, on account of that same gift, he himself justifies us." [66]

This powerful idea came to him at some time during the lectures on Psalms and seized him with gripping force. He has not yet experienced its full implications nor is he yet able to give it adequate expression. Here as elsewhere in his early work he uses the scholastic terminology, *iustitia, iustificatio, gratia,* but it is evident that he is assigning new meanings to the terms. It must not be forgotten that behind the theological refinements of scholastic differentiation as used by Luther in this and the subsequent course of lectures there lies a profoundly real thing, the recognition in the soul of the young scholar of a new discovery. This discovery was a profound inner experience which came perhaps only slowly to his consciousness, and it was as natural for him to formulate it in the hair-split refinements of scholastic phrase as it was for Newton to express the law of gravity in mathematical formulas.

[65] Cf. regarding this question Strohl, *op. cit.,* II, 155ff.
[66] *Ficker,* 2, 66, 4ff.

Stripped of these refinements, the lectures on the Psalter show two great leitmotifs: the consoling power of humility before God and the saving power of faith. As yet, to be sure, the modern Catholic critic finds in his teaching no clear grounds for the charge of heresy.[67] As yet, the Christian still stands in a legal relation before God; "satisfaction through works" still plays its rôle. Purgatory is still a necessary stage. In the search for the means of self-justification, physical means of self-discipline and asceticism are still stressed as necessary. It is recognized, however, that this comes spiritually through man's arraignment of himself, when in debasement before God he recognizes his liability to punishment.[68] Justification consists less in *doing* than in *suffering* that which is imposed upon us, in entrusting ourselves to a merciful God. Through faith the believer testifies to his complete subjection to God's judgment and through faith he takes hold of the mercy of God and His promised forgiveness.

Here, as has been pointed out, the ardent seeker got hold of a thread which led from St. Paul through Augustine and many later scholars and ardent souls of the Middle Ages. But it had tended to become lost in the maze of scholastic refinements and the mechanism of cloister practice. Subjection of self which

---

[67] Denifle, *op. cit.*, I, 441; Grisar, *op. cit.*, I, 56; Christiani, 26, 34: "most orthodox"; only Imbert de la Tour, III, 25: "the equilibrium between the doctrine of grace and works is broken."

[68] *WA*, III, 25.

Luther had known as a normal part of the daily life of his order now appears in another light—subjection to a merciful judgment. The faith in the *caritas* which makes man worthy and pleasing to God now becomes a recognition of God's mercy. Well indeed might the despair of becoming perfect before God which tormented him in the cloister now appear as a normal condition which God Himself desires of the sinner. The chasm which formerly separated him as a sinner from justification closes up when he realizes that man is a sinner and justified at the same time: *the just man lives by faith.*

VII

THE LECTURES ON ROMANS

THE lectures on Psalms extended through two years and marked a long step in the development of the young professor. As has been pointed out, they show us a young theologian inexperienced in exegesis, but with a rich personal religious experience. He seeks to interpret the words of the Hebrew singer, not in a literal sense but in accordance with the hermeneutic practice of his time, as prophecies of Christ. Within this framework he unrolls the whole plan of God for man's salvation. He rests firmly on scholastic authority, and Catholic students still find no heresy in him. But from the very beginning his occupation with the Bible text in order to explain it to his students has been connected, as the evidence seems to show, with a revolution which made God's justice appear to him in an altogether new light. Somewhere in his preparation of these lectures it dawned upon him that man faces not a God of vengeance, but a God of merciful judgments who invites us to entrust ourselves to Him. This great inner experience developed out of an academic investigation and he sought in his lectures to express it in the formulas of his school. His assertions are often self-contradictory, as we seek to trace in *glossae, vocabularia* and *scholia* the lines of development. But the idea is there and shows itself struggling for expression throughout the long, long course of lectures.

Luther himself was quite well aware of the incompetence of this first exegetical course as an interpretation of his theology. "Trifles, quite worthy of being destroyed," he writes to his friend Spalatin at the end of the year,[1] in looking back upon the completed course on the Psalter; and in quaint phrase he denies to these lectures the right to be set in good type by skillful printers. We need not take this disclaimer altogether seriously. He must have felt a triumphant sense of increased power in exegetical technique when he reviewed the development of his views in the Psalms lectures; for when he wrote the letter referred to he was already well advanced with another course, which was to demonstrate how great his progress had been in the past year in clarity of inner vision, originality of view and reliance on his own opinions. For this second course of Wittenberg lectures, that on the Epistle to the Romans, preparatory studies had been begun long before the conclusion of the course on Psalms.

The Romans lectures, as they lie to view in the

[1] Dec. 26, 1515 (*Enders*, I, 27).

National Library in Berlin in Luther's handwriting, are a truly marvelous example of the bibliophilic traditions of the medieval monastic university. The Latin text of Paul's Epistle was printed from the Vulgate in a special edition for this course, the printer allowing a full centimeter between the lines and a broad margin. Here appear the interlinear and marginal notes of the glossary, which are then followed by the long excursus or *scholia* suggested by the text, all marked by meticulous care in initialing and underscoring in red ink. In addition, the Vatican Library contains, in all probability owing to the collector's zeal of the great Protestant Maecenas of the second half of the sixteenth century, Ulrich Fugger of Augsburg, a student's copy of the original.[2] There are also in existence various abstracts of Luther's dictation in the lecture room, though brief indeed as compared with the tremendous preparatory work just described.

The course opened about Easter, 1515, and continued until the end of the summer semester of 1516.[3] Of its popularity we have abundant evidence. "The students liked to hear him, for no one like him had been heard there who translated so boldly every Latin word," declares John Oldecop of Hildesheim, later a bitter enemy of Luther, who registered at the university just as the memorable course opened.[4]

---

[2] Cf. *Ficker*, I, XXX; Stauber, *Das Haus Fugger*, 1900, p. 119.

[3] Cf. Oldecop, *Chronik*, 47; *Ficker*, 1, XLVI.   [4] Oldecop, *op. cit.*, 128.

The lecturer kept within the scholastic framework, but broke down the barriers of tradition by using his mother tongue in order to come nearer to the hearts of his hearers. The use of German increased as the lectures progressed, a fact of national significance, for Luther was in all probability the first German to make free use of his mother tongue from the academic platform and the course on Romans was the first course of which we know which employed the vernacular to interpret a Bible text. Of equal importance is the fact that we have here for the first time in a German university the use of the basic original text of the New Testament. After the ninth chapter Luther has constant recourse to Erasmus' Greek text.

These innovations are matched by an inner boldness and originality which give to the Romans lectures an unique place in theological history and make them in the rugged individuality of their Latin style vividly interesting reading, even to a generation which has lost taste for the fine distinctions of Scholasticism. To begin with, a solid foundation of learning lies at their base. The young professor demonstrates fully his acquaintance with earlier exegetes—Thomas, Peter Lombard, Paul of Burgos and their successors, and the father of Western European exegetes, whom he had used so freely in interpreting the Psalter, Faber Stapulensis. But with the bold spirit of Humanism he goes past earlier interpretations straight to the sources. Alexander's edition of the Aldine Greek lexicon stands at his elbow. Reuchlin's Hebrew grammar is used with increasing independence. After Chapter ix Erasmus' Greek New Testament gives him the basic text, for Greek is no longer a mystery to him. To a modern philologian it is a joy to see how, armed with this increasingly adequate equipment, he attacks the text and displays a fine technique in observation and combination and in the use of his grammatical and logical apparatus to interpret the sense of the original. But what modern scholar could match with him in the philologian's greatest asset, a powerful memory! For it is truly astounding—and only to be explained by the training of an age poor in books—to note the facility with which he quotes, evidently from memory, not merely the Bible, but Augustine and the other Church Fathers, classical and post-classical writers like Seneca and Aesop, mystics like St. Bernard and Tauler, and scholasts like Scotus and Occam.[5] His outlook is not limited by the academic field but he boldly seeks illustrations in the world of contemporary politics, and a popular note rings now and then, culminating in an expression of tavern-table coarseness, strangely out of place amid philosophical arguments or skirmishes with the subtle weapons of dialectics.

Of all sources it is chiefly Augustine who stands at his elbow, Augustine, who as Luther recalls, laid his

[5] Cf. *Ficker*, 1, LV.

conversion to the Epistle to the Romans.[6] Here it is
the work *On the Spirit and the Letter* which chains
his attention and which he recalled in the year before
his death as having contributed to the discovery of the
gospel.[7] Even the language of the African Father
seems at times reflected in Luther's rugged Latin.[8]

The ground tone of the lectures is their author's
attitude toward sin. Particularly Augustine's wonderful psychology of sin, which possibly attracted
Luther's attention and first drew him to this Father of
the Church seven years earlier in Erfurt, now sets its
stamp upon the entire thought of the lectures on
Romans. It rings like an opening chord in the first
sentence of the *scholia:* "The sum and substance of
this Epistle is to destroy and scatter all wisdom and
justice of the flesh . . . and to set fast and confirm
and magnify sin." [9] The actuality and danger of sin
runs like a ruddy thread through the whole. A somber tone marks the young professor's discussion of the
subject and in his presentation of God's attitude
toward the sinner he speaks with the stern accents of
a Jeremiah.[10] God does not desire sin, but wills that
it shall take place in order to manifest to man the

[6] xiii, 13; *Ficker*, 1, 119, 30.

[7] Strohl finds Augustine cited one hundred and twenty-four times in the
lectures; *De spiritu et litera*, twenty-six times. Luther published this work
in 1518. *L'épanouissement de la pensée réligieuse de Luther*, Strasbourg,
1926, 100.

[8] *Ficker*, 1, LXII, notes especially the influence of the *Confessions* on
Luther's language in the *scholia*.

[9] *Ficker*, 2, 1.   [20] Grisar, *op. cit.*, I, 150.

greatness of His nature. The shadow of his struggles in the monastery had not yet lifted from the soul of the exegete and no ray of God as kindly guide and the source of inexhaustible goodness shows itself across the lectures. Sin remains unconquerable even by believers. Even the saints themselves are both just and unjust. In reality they are sinners, but in the eyes of a merciful God they are just, for God considers them according to His mercy. "For behold, every saint is a sinner and prays for his sins. Thus the just man begins with accusation of self." [11]

It is not sin alone, but the very inclination to sin which is incurable. "It is an error to think that this evil is cured by works, since experience proves that in spite of all our good works this desire for evil endures and no one is free from it, not even a day-old child. But such is the mercy of God that although this evil persists, it is not counted as sin to those who call upon God and demand their deliverance with sighs and tears." [12] The sinner is like a patient to whom the doctor has promised recovery. He is still ill in fact, but thanks to the formal promise of his physician in whom he has confidence he may be considered as safe. Luther pictures the dreadful distress in which

---

[11] *"Iustus in principio ist accusator sui* (Ficker, 2, 105, 30). This is, as we have seen, a favorite expression of Luther at this period. It occurs in the lectures on Psalms (WA, III, 29, 16, XXXI., 3 ff.) and in Luther's letters to Spalatin (Feb. 15, 1518; Enders, I, 154; cf. Loofs, *op. cit.*, 415). For the following, cf. the *scholia*, IV, 7, and *passim.*

[12] *Ficker*, 2, 107.

he lived when he could not understand why his sins were not remitted, though God had promised to pardon those who believe in Him: "Not knowing that the pardon is real, but not identical with the suppression of sin" (*"remissio quidem vera sit sed tamen non sit ablatio"*).

He turns savagely against his former teachers who held that man may be led to God by his own natural powers (*"facere quod in se est"*). "Be men!" he calls to them. "Try to do what you say and love God with all your strength by natural forces without grace. If you are then without evil desires, one will believe you." Modern critics have shown that these attacks on the freedom of the human will and the natural powers of man, theories which Luther developed further in the Wittenberg disputation of September 25, 1516, were not justified by Thomas or Bonaventure or by the leaders of high Scholasticism. The men against whom he rails, "O stupids! O pig-theologians!" (*"O stulti! O Sautheologen!"*) for their belief that man can love God above all things by his own powers and that he can accomplish all the works prescribed by the law, these men were really the leaders of the *via moderna*.[13]

It is really on Augustine that Luther reconstructs his conception of the will. Nothing is good for us, but good things are evil because we have sin. "We ought therefore to flee the good and take upon our-

<hr>

[13] Cf. Grisar, *Op. cit.*, I, 164.

selves the evil, and this not with words and pretence alone, but with full desire to declare and choose to be lost and damned. For just as he acts who hates another, so we should act toward ourselves. For whoever hates sincerely, seriously desires to destroy and kill and condemn him whom he hates. If therefore with a sincere heart we shall lose and pursue ourselves, if we shall offer ourselves into hell on account of God and His justice, already in truth we shall satisfy that justice and He will have mercy upon us and set us free." [14]

It is also on Augustine that he leans when he portrays with great vividness the necessity for sin,[15] in that the Christian may not fall into the slough of self-satisfaction. "The mother of all hypocrites and the cause of hypocrisy is security. God leaves us a prey to sin, to a tendency to evil, to concupiscence, in order to maintain us in fear and humility." [16] Indeed in the earlier part of the lectures, morality and humility appear on almost every page. God does not wish that we shall ever cease to have recourse to His grace.

For his imagery to describe man's inclination to sin he lays the Sacred Fathers under contribution and borrows classical examples from the Humanists. It is a law of the flesh, a law of our members, a weakness of nature, a moral illness affecting not only one of the sinner's members, but a weakness which seizes all of his members and diminishes all his forces. "Sin

[24] *Ficker*, 2, 220, 15ff.   [15] Cf. Strohl, *op. cit.*, II, 36.   [36] *Ficker*, 2, 116.

is a hydra of innumerable heads, a monster against which we fight in the Lernian marshes of this life, a Cerberus which barks without ceasing, an Antaeus who is unconquerable on earth."

What then is the way out? Here experience and Augustine have combined to provoke a complete break with his scholastic masters. Scotus and Occam had emphasized the necessity for individual exertion in order to render oneself worthy of grace and thus rise to a love of God devoid of self. Occamism also, as we have seen, had emphasized the sovereignty of God, who accepts man's merits quite irrationally without His judgment being subject to any law. Out of these ideas Luther may have deduced the conception of an irrational love of God and of the enslaved will *(servum arbitrium)*. His Occamist teachers had passed on to Luther these voluntarist and irrational ideas, which had developed in the preceding century as a reaction against the scholastic identification of God with justice. Augustine's powerful arguments against the Pelagians armed Luther to break with his school on the subject of the natural powers of man; but it was the school itself which supplied him with the idea of God's arbitrary predestination and man's enslaved will. Our only salvation lies in abject humiliation, the only merit which we can claim is the fear of God. "Why does man have pride in his merits and his works, which are in no way pleasing because they are good or have merit,

but because they have been elected by God of eternity
to please Him? . . . Not our works make us good,
but our good nature, nay rather the good nature of
God makes us and our works good. Because they are
not good in themselves nor unless God reputes them
to be good. . . . Whoever understands this is ever in
fear, ever fearing and expecting the imputation of
God." [17] "Happy is he alone," Luther quotes from
Job, "who is always in fear," [18] for how can we be
sure that the good within us comes from God? How
can we know that our deeds please God? Away with
the self-righteous who are so sure of their good
works! Let the man who goes to confession not believe that he is rid of his burden. Sin remains to
exercise us in the life of grace, to humiliate our pride
and check our presumption."

The only salvation then is in the broken will and
humbled heart, ready to accept what God imposes.
Works avail naught, for the supreme will of God has
decided to save us, not by our own righteousness, but
by extraneous righteousness, by the imputed righteousness of Christ.

At the beginning of the course of lectures, the
professor is not ready to proclaim assurance of salvation. "We are never able to know whether we are
justified," he declares,[19] but by degrees the confidence
that God will care for the future becomes more and
more outspoken. If we sink ourselves into nothing-

[17] *Ficker*, 2, 221.   [18] *Ficker*, 2, 323.   [19] *Ficker*, 2, 88, 32ff.

ness, we shall placate God and receive the imputed righteousness of Christ: "In our ignorance justified, in our knowledge unjustified." [20]   Not yet, to be sure, is his soul fully lighted by faith, although he ascribes a high place to faith in comparison with works. Predestination, about which his remarks are not altogether clear, still causes him anxiety.[21]   It is certain that God's elect will be saved, but no one can be sure that *he* will be chosen. Humility must go to the point where the sinning soul is willing to accept eternal damnation because it is the will of God: "For such as offer themselves freely to the will of God in all, even to hell and eternal punishment if God wishes, in order that His will may be fully done." [22]   But he comforts himself with a dialectical demonstration of the impossibility that such a soul should be lost. He wishes what God wishes, therefore he pleases God; if he pleases Him, then he is loved; if he is loved, then he must be saved.[23]   In a contemporary letter Luther supports this thesis with an old parable: the sinner simply casts himself upon Christ and hides as under the wings of a hen. Catholic critics have contended that there is something mechanical in such a plan of justification as opposed to the organic inner workings of grace.

It cannot be denied that to the modern reader there is a somberness in Luther's presentation of sin

[20] *Iniusti in re; iusti in spe.*
[21] *Ficker, 2, 217, 18ff.*
[22] *Ficker, 2, 212, 217.*
[23] *Ficker, 2, 218.*

and justification that has something of the gloom of medieval asceticism. Nor can it be denied that there are uncertainties in his theological position, particularly as regards predestination. But the lectures in this very phase, with their intense eloquence and lurid flashes of temperamental vehemence, reflect the soul battles through which he had passed. Indeed, he reënacts these struggles before us in theological costume. The fearful despair, the power of the Evil One and the impotence of human effort, the struggle for security, and the swaying back and forth between certainty and uncertainty of salvation, are all leaves plucked from the book of his cloister life. Through all runs the breathless eagerness of the fighter. "We are not called to ease, but to labor against our passions." [24] The law of our life is a combat and a fight. "It is thus that we learn to love God with a pure and disinterested love, not on account of grace and gifts, but on account of God himself."[25] "Who would think this life a path of peace when he sees Christians vexed in affairs, in reputation, in the body and having their life long not peace but the cross and suffeffring? . . . Amid these very things peace lies hid, but no one recognizes it save him who believes and experiences it." [26] Thus suffering becomes a school of faith.

With justice a modern editor aligns the spirit of the work with that of Erasmus' *Manual of the Christian Soldier* and Dürer's painting of the knight riding un-

[24] *Ficker*, 2, 178, 34.   [25] *Ficker*, 2, 137, 14.   [26] *Ficker*, 2, 83, 12ff.

afraid between death and the devil. The monk professor had fought his battle with the teachers of his youth and finished with them. Augustine and his own experience have henceforth given him a new orientation. His guiding theses have become: the hereditary sinfulness of mankind, the nothingness of the human will, and the imputation of the righteousness of Christ, assuring a grace which has in it nothing of the magic character so naturally and frequently associated with the sacrament, but which is a liberating force. Predestination still remains an anxious spot, and he has not yet brought himself to express the unqualified certainty of salvation. Nor has faith as yet won a permanent and commanding place in his mind beside humility.

Next to the influence of Augustine on the development of Luther's thought as expressed in the lectures on Romans stands that of the German mystics. Already in his earlier theological studies in the Erfurt cloister he had formed the acquaintance of such practical mystics as Bernard of Clairvaux, Bonaventure and Gerson. In these writers he had found an ideal of cloister piety that springs from a deep humiliation of the soul before God, and it is this profound sinking of self into nothing before God's majesty which we saw expressed in the lectures on the Psalter,[27] and which runs as a basic motive through the Romans lectures and later appears in the powerful appeals of

[27] Cf. Braun, *op. cit.*, 51ff.

the *Sermon on Good Works* and the pamphlet *On the Monk's Vow*. The strongly emotional nature of Luther could not fail to throb in unison with the conception of humility so powerfully set forth by Augustine and Bernard, and from his first acquaintance with these authors he must have found in their ideals of humility a powerful counter-irritant to the rationalistic refinements of Occam and his school.

It may have been through Staupitz that Luther made acquaintance with the text of the youngest of the German mystic fathers, Johann Tauler. Possibly as early as the summer of 1515 [28] he had in his hand a copy of sermons by the great Dominican who almost two centuries before had thrilled the Alsatian cloisters with appeals for a life freed from self through the fusion of the soul by love with the perfect soul of God. Almost immediately the glowing eloquence of the Strassburg monk threw its spell over him and found reflection in the Romans lectures.[29] "I have never," he writes to Spalatin soon after the conclusion of the lectures,[30] "either in Latin or our language seen a theology which was saner and more in accord with the Evangelists." Indeed, throughout the years 1516 and 1517 when the ideas which later show such explosive force were crystallizing into form he comes back to Tauler again and again in his correspondence with his friends and urges the importance of the ser-

---

[28] *WA*, IX, 95; cf. Strohl, *L'épanouissement*, II, 114.
[29] *Ficker*, 2, 205, 21ff.   [30] Dec. 14, 1516 (*Enders*, I, 75).

mons of the Strassburg mystic. The throbbing eloquence of Tauler's style set its stamp on the style of
his correspondence at this time. A copy of the sermons of Tauler, marked with comments and annotations probably from the year 1516, formed a permanent part of his library.[31] Many passages in the
Romans lectures seem to show the influence of this
one of the fathers of German prose. Thus, for in-
stance, when he tells his students that God's righteousness fills only those who seek to empty themselves of
their own righteousness.[32]

Two ideas of Tauler stand out in the Romans lectures in especial relief: the passive reception of God
by the Christian and the necessity for loving God
without egotistic motives.

The only way to God lies through suffering. The
soul must "endure God" (*"Gott leiden"*), a thought
which Luther stresses later in his marginal notes on
Tauler's sermons.[33] Without suffering, the soul
languishes. It no longer seeks God, no longer thirsts
for God, the source of life. "O how gladly we are
empty, that Thou mayst be full in us! How gladly
weak, that Thy virtue may dwell strong within me!
How gladly a sinner, that Thou mayst be just within
me; how gladly ignorant, that Thou mayst be my
wisdom; how gladly unjust, that Thou mayst be my

[31] *WA*, IX, 97-104.

[32] *Ficker*, 2, 59, 5ff.; cf. 135; Grisar, *op. cit.*, I, 132ff.; A. V. Müller,
Luther und Tauler, passim.

[33] *WA*, IX, 97.

justice!" [34] The same idea appears later in the *Ninety-five Theses*, and the *Sermon on Good Works* (1520) is filled with the conception of unceasing discipline through God.[35]

In Tauler he also finds set forth in impassioned tones the demand that the Christian love God unselfishly, without hope of reward. This idea plays an important rôle in the Romans lectures, where Luther recasts Tauler's flaming eloquence on the subject in his own somber but vigorous language. The soul must love God to the point where it desires that the will of God be done even if that means its own condemnation to the eternal fires,[36] an idea compounded of baffling predestination concepts and mystic ecstasy. This idea of voluntary and selfless love and service is further developed in the *Sermon on Good Works* and gives rise to one of the most powerful passages in the *Freedom of a Christian Man* (par. 26-29).

Perhaps in 1516 he came across the incomplete manuscript of the *Theologia Germanica* a tract by an unknown author belonging to the springtime of German mysticism, the middle of the fourteenth century. It is written with rare simplicity of style and in a German the quaint, archaic flavor of which must have been as sweet to Luther's palate as the old-fashioned periods of John Bunyan are to the English reader of the twentieth century. He assumed that the books was written by Tauler and read with eager-

[34] *Ficker*, 2, 59, 5. [35] Cf. Strohl, *op. cit.*, II, 132. [36] *Ficker*, 2, 215-219.

ness the simple and devout rhapsodies concerning the nature of God and life in Him of those who really love God. He thereupon immediately wrote a little introduction to the work and had it printed in Wittenberg. This first edition, also Luther's first printed work,[37] was followed two years later by the publication of the complete work, which had then come into his hands.[38] A formidable group of foreign scholars —Windstosser, Mandel, A. V. Müller among them— hold that this book by the so-called "Frankforter" was of decisive influence in determining Luther's ideas. They are of the opinion that the *Theologia Germanica* led Martin to Paul and therefore contributed largely to the shaping of Protestant faith. This would mean that the reading of the work fell early in the Wittenberg years. There is, however, no reference to it in the Romans lectures.

No matter when the *Theologia Germanica* first came into his hands, there can be no doubt that the intense study of these two authors of mystical prose was of great aid to Luther in these crucial years. In contrast with the rationalistic dialectics of the Nominalists and the stern, uncompromising conception of man's sin and God's righteousness which he found in Augustine, they showed him the way out of the night of the soul which often enveloped him. In them he found repose in self-humiliation before God. Here he learned that the soul by filling itself with the sense

[37] *WA*, I, 152.   [38] *WA*, I, 378ff.

of its own infinite nothingness can prepare for a complete union with God, and that a state of terror may itself be the forerunner of the dawning light of a joyous faith.   The reading of these books formed also an important counterbalance to the narrow Humanism which might have contracted his work within the strait-jacket of an academic Latinity. Thus far his theological authorities had been those of the learned language of scholarship.   In the Mystics he found deeply religious thought clothed in eloquent German, and it is during his occupation with these works that German words filter more and more into the lectures which he dictated.

In the Romans lectures there rises to view for the first time the note of bold independence and individualism which increasingly marks his work from now on.   His surroundings and development have armed him with a strong spirit of individualism. "Let each one," he demands in his early lectures, "be strong in his own conscience" (*"uniusquisque robustus sit in conscientia tua"*).   He is, to be sure, still a monk, and shows in the tone of the lectures many traits of the monkish spirit of the later Middle Ages— a deep soulfulness and mystic longing for God, mingled strangely with a certain uncouth rationalism and here and there an irrepressible coarseness of tone. However, he already turns on the whole monkish observance a critical eye, emphasizing repeatedly the corruption of the Church as shown by the Pope and the chief prelates who stand between the Christian people and the true sonship of God. Popes and bishops, he affirms, are more cruel than cruelty itself, refusing to grant for God's sake indulgence for sin which they have received for nothing. In a tone of prophetic boldness he charges these "corrupt and abominable ones," themselves "led astray," with "leading astray the people of Christ from the true worship of God." [39]   In a vigorous excursus he turns to the conflict between the civil and canonical law, at that time a theme of consuming interest, and the abuse of the power of excommunication in the assertion of ecclesiastical claims to property and privilege. "There may be doubt, but it merely seems to me that the secular powers to-day exercise their office more happily and better than the ecclesiastical. For they punish rigidly theft and murder, save in so far as they are hindered by tricky laws. But the ecclesiastics, while damning only those who invade the liberties, powers and rights of the church, nourish rather than punish works of pride, ambition, indulgence and strife." [40]

Finally he charges the ecclesiastical hierarchy with the whole catalog of vices which the Apostle lists in II Timothy iii. Like every reformer after the tenth century, he is aroused by the sordid materialism of the clergy, to which he returns again and again: "These stupid and godless ecclesiastics who strut

[39] *Ficker*, 2, 243, 21.   [40] *Ficker*, 2, 300, 10ff.

about with the goods which they have received from the laity and think that they are doing enough when they mutter a few prayers on behalf of their benefactors"; and he voices, like many of his German contemporaries, the conviction that "it would certainly be better if the temporal affairs of the clergy also were placed under the secular power . . . if they had also to fear others, to that extent they would also be more cautious in everything." [41]

More and more as the lectures approach their end he raises his voice against the heads of the Church, and refers to contemporary events to motivate his anger. The pending effort of the city of Strassburg to bring a criminal canon to justice,[42] the chronic struggle between the Bishop of Brandenburg and the city council of Wittenberg, the rivalry between the Elector of Saxony and the Archbishop of Mainz in the acquisition of sacred relics and the local traffic in indulgences, which had reached a point to cause consternation in Wittenberg and its vicinity—all these and many other questions of the day he lays before his students to illustrate his arraignment of the higher clergy. Especially the sale of indulgences was becoming an acute question and involved Luther's own monastery, the buildings for which were rising in the year of his lectures on Romans. The usual method of raising money for such purposes was through the

---

[41] *Ficker*, 2, 300, 15 ff.; cf. Grisar, *op. cit.*, I, 283.

[42] Cf. Röhricht, *Geschichte der Reformation im Elsass*, I, 41.

issue of new indulgences, and two papal bulls author-
izing these were published in 1516, one for the building of the church of St. Peter in Rome and the other
for the completion of All Saints Church in Wittenberg.

It is not only the Curia and prelates whom he arraigns for corruption, luxury, pride, ambition and
sacrilege. The whole life of the Church suffers from
an excess of observance. "If you do not believe that
you have safety anywhere else than in the religious
life," he warns, "do not enter it, for the proverb is
true that desperation makes the monk, nay, not a
monk but rather a devil. For no one will have become a good monk who has become a monk through
desperation, but he who has become one from love
and from seeing his own sins and wishing to do something great for his God through love, voluntarily re-
signs his liberty and puts on the stupid dress and
subjects himself to lowly duties." [43]

[43] *Ficker*, 2, 318, 5.

VIII

THE FINAL BREAK WITH SCHOLASTICISM

At the close of the year 1516 Luther's convictions on theological questions were still undergoing development. He was still a devoted son of the Church, proclaiming her divine mission to teach and save, and he was eager that she might purify herself of her errors. His theological studies were far from complete and regarding many points he was still uncertain. He had concluded his course of lectures on Romans, with its presentation of the awfulness of sin and its deeply mystical conception of God's power and man's nothingness, without being able to assure the repentant sinner of the certainty of salvation; at least the arguments which have been adduced to show that he did are far from convincing.[1] On the last day of 1517 he can still write to his friend Spalatin that he does not regard calling on the saints as a superstition and that it is better to get good things through a saint than through a devil or by magic.[2]

Nevertheless, he has won for himself an independent position regarding the great question of justifica-

[1] Cf. below, pp. 209, 216.   [2] *Enders*, I, 135.

tion and its ancillary problems of merit, good works and the ability of the human soul to do things pleasant to God. His ideas of grace, powerful and explosive as they were, were not clear to him in some of their implications. Resting on profound soul experiences and deriving their force from deep sources of vital energy within him, they still had in his mind the form of academic propositions which were to be fought over in the arena of the disputation. Full certainty regarding justification does not seem to have come until the last year of his intensive occupation with St. Paul's theology as set forth in the Epistle to the Romans. His letters at this time are filled with echoes of the Pauline studies on which he was engaged. He criticizes those who seek through good works to stand before God, "decked as it were, with their virtues and merits." "I too," he recalled, "was in this error and still struggle against it and have not get overcome it." [3] It is in the tone of a seeker, not yet sure of his ground, that he urges another Augustinian brother in his old cloister of Erfurt to appeal to his former teacher Usingen for relief from the temptations which surround him, reminding him that all trouble comes from the wisdom of our own minds. [4] Six months later, following the conclusion of the Romans lectures, Luther's tone has grown firmer. Works performed outside of faith, he writes,

[3] To George Spenlein, April 8, 1519 (*Enders*, I, 29).
[4] To George Leiffer, April 15, 1516 (*Enders*, I, 31).

have as little to do with righteousness "as blackberries with figs." [5]

At the beginning of the year which was to bring him out of his cell, lecture room and refectory into the great arena of public combat, Luther has at last built up a system of justification which he henceforth maintains with extraordinary tenacity. Its foundations were laid, as we have seen, on the basis of the doctrine of the all-powerful, irrational will of God as he received it in Occam's school. He has built into it something of St. Augustine's views of the fusion between will and faith and especially the African Father's mystical conception of the overwhelming importance of Christ's life and passion for man's salvation. German mystics have filled him with their ideas of the suffering soul cast down into nothingness before God. In St. Paul he has discovered a truly overwhelming conception of God as the personification of love, and of faith as the great bond which assures to man the non-imputation of sin. These ideas he has not accepted merely as intellectual concepts but has welded them into an intense personal conviction through his fiery struggles for peace of soul. They form a platform upon which he dragged himself up out of the black waters of despair.

Let us review for a moment the system of Luther's convictions as they appear in the lectures on Romans. In doing this we make no claim to an exhaustive

[5] To Spalatin, October 19, 1516 (*Enders*, I, 64).

analysis of Luther's theology as it appears in the later works and as it has been set forth as a chapter of the history of dogma by such scholars as Seeberg, or in an apologetic framework by Karl Holl, or critically and destructively by Denifle, Jundt and others. The idea of building a *system* of theology was certainly absent from Luther's mind in preparing his lectures on Romans, indeed it may be doubted whether he was ever consciously a systematist any more than he was a church historian. But the year 1517 could not have played the rôle in religious history that it did had Luther not first battled his way to clarity regarding the fundamental articles of his faith, nor could the monk have come to actual grips with a solidly founded system of theology if his own system had not by this time been built upon a solid foundation. The ideas set forth in the lectures on Romans are essentially the reformatory ideas of the years 1517 to 1520, although not yet clad in the form for combat which they were to assume in these years.

The lectures on Romans, therefore, even though they do not contain a complete abstract of theology, at least present the bald outlines of one. God appears in them, not as a God of law but as a God of love and mercy, who overwhelms us with His kindness, "for His glory consists in his graciousness to us." [6] The chief of His mercies is that He does not impute our sins to us. Through contact with God

[6] *Ficker*, 2, 339, 19.

man undergoes a change and experiences a work of healing which is to go on forever. God picks him up half-alive as the Good Samaritan did the man by the wayside, a favorite image with Luther. Through our suffering in the school of temptation we find Him. In inspired language Luther pictures to us a God who is mysterious and terrible and at the same time a God of love. His majesty surpasses our intelligence, and the lecturer rails at those who speak of God with the same readiness and the same lack of respect as the shoemaker of his leather.[7] The terrible idea of predestination itself drives us always back to God for aid and safety. It quite destroys man's presumption and but for this refuge would leave him face to face with solitary despair.

Sin appears with a lurid light across the pages of the lectures on Romans. Sin is to Luther the greatest reality in life, and his chief fear is of heresies like Pelagianism which lead men to trust in natural goodness and to forget their own unworthiness. In the face of such a conception of sin Luther hesitates to speak with definiteness of the absolute certainty of salvation; but he points out that hope and faith are identical and that God's promises inspire the hope that the non-imputation of sin will last until Judgment. Luther urges the believer to cast himself boldly on God's promises: "If anyone should fear that he is not chosen or be tempted regarding his

[7] *"Wie der Schuster vom Leder"* (Ficker, 2, 27, 2-7).

election . . . let him hurl himself with boldness upon the God of Promise . . . and he will be safe." [8]

How much Luther's conception of God in 1517 was affected by the reading of the *Theologia Germanica* and of Tauler is a matter of opinion. It should be pointed out, however, that there are very essential differences between the conception of God developed in the German mystical writers of the fourteenth century and Luther's position as revealed in the Romans lectures and the sermons and tractates of 1517 to 1520. The absolute character of God as it appears in the mystical literature of a Tauler is a sort of philosophical concept with strongly Neo-Platonic implications. This opens the way to that ecstatic and aristocratic cultivation of the ego which delights in soul analysis and in the emotional metaphysics quite familiar to the readers of these works.[9] This was entirely foreign to Luther's realistic conception of an awakened conscience and Christian duty. Nevertheless, as we have seen, mystical ideas which are quite definitely Tauler's are strongly developed in the religious pattern which Luther works out in the lectures on Romans. He dwells with eagerness on the conception of "enduring God" so important to Tau-

---

[8] "*In veritatem promittentis Dei audacter ruat . . . et salvus erit*" (Ficker, II, 214, 27ff.). Karl Holl, *Gesammelte Aufsätze zur Kirchengeschichte*, I, Luther, 1923, regards the certainty of salvation as clearly implied in the lectures on Romans, but his arguments are too fine-spun to be convincing as against the quite definite statements in Luther's *scholia*. Cf. below, p. 216.

[9] Cf. Holl, *op. cit.*, 12.

ler and the author of the *Theologia Germanica*, who urge us not to force God, but to wait till God forces us, until our will unites with the divine will. The mysticism of Tauler and the Frankforter is orthodox in that it does not lead to independence of the sacraments, but it nevertheless did lead the young teacher away from the arid speculations of theology to look deep within his own soul for God, to feel him, to taste him there.[10] We find in Luther's lectures on Romans, as in Tauler, a resignation of the will, a love of God without self-interest or egotism, ideas which reappear in the *Sermon on Good Works* in 1520.[11] Undoubtedly the psychological condition of passivity, the twilight zone of consciousness when the soul is relaxed and obedient, had shown itself in Luther's own religious experience, as in that of Tauler and the author of the *Theologia Germanica*, as favorable for the reception of powerful religious impressions. "For the first grace and as it were, for glory, let us always hold ourselves as passive as the woman for conception. For we are also the spouse of Christ. So it is permitted that beforehand we should pray and entreat for grace, nevertheless when grace comes and the soul is impregnated with the Spirit, it is proper that no prayers should be uttered, but that we should

[10] K. Müller, *Kritische Beiträge*, III. "*Sitzungsberichte der Berliner Akademie der Wiss.*," 1919, pp. 654ff.; Seeberg, *Dogmengeschichte*, III, 561ff.

[11] A. V. Müller, *Luther und Tauler*, Chs. III, IV; cf. Strohl, *op. cit.*, II, 120ff. Müller has shown that the *Leitmotiv* in the *Freiheit eines Christenmenschen* is to be found almost exactly in Tauler.

only suffer." [12] The necessity for suffering as a therapeutic element in the Christian life, so essential to the thought of these predecessors of Luther, is expressed in a number of passages in the lectures on Romans,[13] as well as in the *Sermon on Good Works*, and in vibrant tones in the last four of the theses against indulgences. Similarly the demand that man seek God, not for the rewards which He has to give but for union with God Himself, is a thought which Luther found in Tauler and the *Theologia Germanica*, and which, as we have seen, he develops with ardor in the lectures on Romans.[14]

That these ideas had a strong influence on Luther's thought in the years 1517-1520 is certain. He opposed to them, however, the realism of an active and strongly rational temperament. He seems never to have yielded to the Neo-Platonism of Augustine, and the same realistic sense kept him from yielding to the Neo-Platonism of the mystical writers. The conception of God as an impenetrable mystery, an abstraction of the Good, ideas which pervaded the German mystical writers, gave way in Luther to a vitalistic conception which was quite different. In his lectures on Psalms in 1513 he affirms that after reading the works of Dionysius the Areopagite he had sought to practice the exercises by which the superman (*vir hierarchius*) of the mystical writers rises in

[12] *Ficker*, 2, 206, 17.   [13] *Ficker*, 2, 160, 29; 161, 20 etc.
[14] Cf. Müller, *Luther und Tauler*, 102.

soul ecstasy through celestial stages to a blessed vision of divine majesty, the "real Cabbala which is very rare." [15] These experiments in an "ecstatic and negative theology," as he calls it, he does not seem to have repeated. His nature was, as has been said, too practical to find satisfaction in such processes of airy speculation.

Nevertheless, the mystic writers of the fourteenth century made a lasting contribution to his religious growth, in spite of the realism which was his distinguishing trait through life. His ardent and enthusiastic nature had been engaged since his first induction into theological study in a desperate and exasperating battle with the rigid abstractions of the schoolmen. In the first stage of this struggle, in the late Erfurt and early Wittenberg years, Augustine came to his support. Here he found a rich life of the soul, a realistic conception of sin and a vivid sense of God, and from there he drew strength for combat with the idea of an avenging Deity. In the second stage of his development, in the succeeding years, the German mystics gave aid to the African Father, with their emphasis on the passivity of the soul in order that it may receive the gift of God, on the necessity for the resignation of the will and of all selfish desires. Having absorbed these ideas Luther was ready to see with the eyes of Paul, not a God of justice, but a God of love.

[15] *WA*, III, 372, 16.

A further development of the ideas in the lectures on Romans is found in two succeeding courses—on the Epistle to the Galatians and the Epistle to the Hebrews. Unfortunately neither is available in a form which enables the student to judge adequately of its contents when delivered, and neither adds significant features to the picture of the religious position of Luther at this time. The lectures on Galatians, commenced October 27, 1516,[16] immediately after the conclusion of the lectures on Romans, were published in 1519, apparently in a revised form.[17] A student's notebook on the lectures, recently found,[18] does not seem to have caught Luther's ideas. In the following spring, 1517, at Easter, Luther began the course on Hebrews, which lasted till Easter, 1518. This exists only in a student's transcript in the Vatican Library. It is still unpublished, although extracts have been made available.[19]

[16] *Enders*, I, 67.

[17] *In epistulam Pauli ad Galatos commentaria* (*WA*, II, 437-618; IX, 790). The situation regarding the lectures on Galatians is especially to be regretted. Luther calls the Epistle, which treats so forcefully of faith, "my epistle in which I have put my trust. It is my Käthie von Bora" (*TR*, I, 146). What we have is a commentary worked over in the stormy year 1519 (*Enders*, II, 12, 63, 139). Luther issued an edition in 1523 and caused a German translation of this to be published in the same year. In 1531 he lectured again on Galatians, and this course became the basis of a new commentary, published by one of his students, Rörer, in 1538 (*WA*, XL, 1 and 2; cf. Schubert, *op. cit.*, VII).

[18] H. v. Schubert, *Vorlesung über Luthers Galaterbrief*, "*Abhandlungen der Heidelberger Akademie*," 1921.

[19] By Joh. Ficker in *Luther, 1917*, "*Schriften des Vereins für Reformationsgeschichte*," CXXX (1918); cf. Meissner, *Luthers Exegese in der Frühzeit*, Leipzig, 1911, p. 21.

Both of these courses are a disappointment to one who comes to them from reading the vigorous Latin of the lectures on Romans. The lectures on Galatians, as we have them, do not bear the stamp of freshness or originality, doubtless because they are a revision, while those on the Epistle to the Hebrews, which have slept so long in the Vatican library, are not as yet sufficiently accessible for us to judge them fairly. Striking is the fact that in neither course do we have any longer the tone of the "seeker," as in the previous lectures, but the decided manner of one who has finally arrived at assurance. In these courses the conviction of the insufficiency of man and all his works to win God's favor is stressed even more decidedly than before, but without the profound originality of expression and eager earnestness of the Romans lectures. "All the works of faith," he declares in the Hebrews course, "are impossible to nature, but they are very easy for grace, because they are done solely by God, while we ourselves remain passive." [20] Here, as in the course on Galatians, looms ever the great contrast between the law and grace, which is, he declares, the very basis of Paul's Epistle to the Hebrews, "against the pride of the righteousness of the law and of man." [21] The law is odious since it demands what cannot be fulfilled. Through it man is rendered worse, not better.[22] It has, to be sure, its pedagogical uses, since it makes the Christian

[20] Ficker, *Luther, 1917*, p. 35.　[21] *Ibid.*, p. 34.　[22] *WA*, II, 525, 7.

realize how far he is from perfection and shows him what he must do in order to retain the grace which he has received, "showing man that grace is due to no merit of his."

In both courses he dwells with proud self-consciousness on the wonderful works of God, who through His spirit in the hearts of men awakens them to charity and good works and makes them victors over every evil, including death.[23] "Faith it is, the faith of man which so exalts the heart of man and transfers it from man himself into God, that his heart and God fuse together into one spirit and thus divine justice becomes the justice of man's own heart."[24]

The tone of definite assurance which marks both courses is especially notable when the lecturer comes to speak of the certainty of salvation. Here he has made a marked advance over the lectures on Romans. It is the duty of the Christian to feel secure, he now proclaims to his students,[25] to force himself to be absolutely assured of his safety through faith in Christ.[26] This is definitely emphasized not only in the two lecture courses, but in a sermon of the same period On the Sacrament of Baptism, 1519.[27] It is, however, a feeling which must be won through a con-

---

[23] WA, II, 536, 30.   [24] Ficker, Luther, 1917, p. 35.
[25] "Christianum . . . oportet semper certum esse" (Scholia, Bl. 102); "Oportet Christianum certum esse, immo certissimum, Christianum pro se apparere et pontificem esse apud Deum" (Scholia, Bl. 121b); cf. Ficker, Luther, 1917, p. 36.
[26] WA, II, 458, 29.   [27] WA, II, 737.

tinual exercise in faith, for the Christian remains, as
it were, suspended between heaven and earth: "In
Christ he hangs crucified in the air." [28]

It was not only in the preparation of his exegetical
lectures that Luther wrought out his religious ideas.
During the first five years of his service in the Wittenberg cloister and university he developed as preacher
the power to attract an audience from among the
cloister brothers, from academic circles and from the
burghers of the city. The religious and moral questions which were discussed in the lectures on Romans
and subsequently find presentation at the same time
in more popular form in the refectory of the convent,
in the city churches of Wittenberg and on at least one
occasion before the representatives of the cloisters of
his order in a district convention. Preaching at that
time was at a low ebb in Germany,[29] as indeed
throughout Europe, and public preachers were found
almost solely in the mendicant orders. Among the
Augustinian monks the selection of the brothers for
the preaching office was not left to the individual
cloisters, but fell within the office of the general
vicar. Luther tells us that his first sermon was before the brethren in the refectory of the convent,[30]
but it is not certain whether he first ascended the
pulpit in his mother cloister or in Wittenberg.[31] In
recalling many years later a memorable conversation

[28] *Scholia*, Bl. 106; Ficker, *Luther*, 1917.   [29] Grisar, *op. cit.*, I, 60.
[30] *TR*, III, 3143b-1532.   [31] Oergel, *op. cit.*, 118; Scheel, *Luther*, II, 308.

with Staupitz under the pear tree in the Wittenberg cloister court, in which the general vicar laid on him the duty of becoming a doctor of philosophy with the office of preaching, Luther remembered his mighty fear of the pulpit and his reluctance to follow the call. It is evident that this feeling was soon overcome, and that in the face of a popular audience he flung himself into the task with fiery enthusiasm.

His sermons in the period before the struggle over indulgences have come down to us, not in the German in which a great part of them were undoubtedly delivered, but in the form of Latin outlines, notes and summaries. From these it is clear that he lit the fires of enthusiasm only after a preparation as careful as that which we have learned to know in the preparation of his academic lectures. When he is getting ready a sermon for St. Bartholomew's Day in the busy August of 1516, he takes time to write to Spalatin, asking him to send him the text of St. Jerome's works in order that he may include in his sermon what Jerome says of the Apostle. The number of sermons that are extant from the first six years of his professorship is astonishingly large. They draw texts from the epistles and gospels of the church year, the Ten Commandments, the Lord's Prayer, they treat of penance, or of the burning questions of indulgences and excommunication. Polemical subjects figure more and more largely until 1519, when Latin goes and German comes in.

This change of language is, indeed, typical for the great transformation from the academic scholar to the public protagonist, which began in 1518 and had reached its completion in the summer of 1520. As the years go by, one may trace the fading of academic, scholastic patterns in the sermons, as the fantastic allegories built up on Bible texts, which formed so important a part of the stock in trade of the preacher of the later Middle Ages, give place to a more simple and practical effort to awaken an inner fear of God and stimulate to good works as an outgrowth of faith. His command of the Scriptures is unlimited and his application of them is constant. His attacks on Church and society were as merciless here as in his academic lectures. It is surprising when one considers the times that the authorities of his order or of the diocese did not find that the tone of his sermons called for intervention. This is in itself evidence of a recognition of Luther's sincerity of character.

The boldness of his tone and his self-confidence were indeed calculated to array enemies against him. There is abundant evidence that an ardent and impulsive temperament and the training which the later Middle Ages gave in the use of a coarse and belligerent tone in theological polemics united to make Luther a rough opponent. Academic disputations, especially those on theological questions, furnished him with models enough for this, and such classical authors as he had read in the Trivial schools were not wanting in strong expressions for attacking hard heads. He had not been long in Wittenberg before he began to turn here and there to German as furnishing more forceful and more easily understood appellations for his opponents, and his selections were made with skill. In an address *On the Little Saints*, delivered in 1515, we find scattered in the Latin text many German epithets. "Poisonous serpents," "traitors," "devils," and similar characterizations are to be found in his lectures on Romans,[32] while in his correspondence the same tone of bitter intolerance and abuse shows itself, here again with a vocabulary quite usual at a time when no tender consideration was shown academic or theological opponents. It is characteristic that to his earnest, theological mind bitter language seemed quite permissible when applied to the enemies of what he held to be the truth, while he could not approve of the biting, often frivolous satire which Humanists like Ulrich von Hutten directed against arrogant Scholasticism. It is not surprising that persons who knew him in these years in looking back from a hostile camp across the bitter struggles that rent the Church should have remembered him as obstinate, presumptuous and quarrelsome.[33] Attacks upon leading authorities in Scholasticism, especially the honored fathers of the *via moderna*, launched by

[32] E.g., *Ficker*, 2, 110, 3.

[33] Grisar, *op. cit.*, I, 18, cites passages; cf. Hausrath, *Luther*, 54.

such a temperamental and ruthless opponent, aroused a feeling of resentment that grew apace as the circle of enemies widened when he transferred his attacks to the temporal authorities of the Church and heaped ridicule on its institutions with puns and frivolous jests, as in the work *On the Monk's Vow*.[34]

Like most men of impulsive temperament, Luther recognized his faults. We have more than one sermon against the vice of contentiousness and quarrelsomeness which reads like a personal confession. He admits the bitter tone of his works and defends himself by saying that he hated a "soft-spoken man."[35] A man who could write a comforting letter to an opponent like Tetzel and show kindness to an intolerant academic rival like Carlstadt was incapable of harboring a grudge. It seems quite certain also that he had nothing of one great vice of the academic world—envy.

The expressions of violence and intolerance did not become marked in his correspondence and writings until after 1517. Nevertheless from the time of the conclusion of the Romans lectures a tone of vigorous denunciation grows apace in his writings. He has pulled himself out of the flood of despair and he looks down from his refuge with bitter contempt on the theological school in which he has been nursed. He proclaims his views with assurance and finds no

[34] Denifle, *op. cit.*, I, 127.
[35] Braun, *Luthers Klostererlebnis*, 14.

words too severe for those who taught that man by his intellectual powers is able to do anything whatever to please God. All human freedom of the will has been dashed from its throne and sin is held aloft as man's natural element. The first of the proud ideals of Scholasticism against which he turns is Aristotle. Already in the lectures on Psalms he had charged the philosopher with bringing a profane and bold worldliness into theology. Now early in 1517 he writes to an Erfurt friend [36] that he is occupied with a commentary on Aristotle's *Physics*. He hopes to tear away the mask from the "mountebank," whose philosophy is a many-headed serpent. In another letter in the following year he attacks the whole system of theology which had adapted the Stagirite to its purposes, and tells his old teacher Trutvetter that Scholasticism and the canon law are both on the same footing and both in need of a thorough reform.[37]

The story of Luther's early religious development has now been told. It would, however, be incomplete did we not take at least a brief glance at the personal transformation wrought in the young professor by the winning of clearness of conviction on the subject of grace and salvation. Almost at once his indomitable energy of purpose drives him to proclaim these convictions outside of the seclusion of the theological lecture and the privacy of correspondence. Certain

---

[36] Lang, Feb. 8 (*Enders*, I, 85).   [37] *Enders*, I, 187, May 9, 1518.

"ban dogs in Wittenberg," he writes in September, 1516,[38] had been "barking" against his lectures on Romans. Luther had no doubt thoroughly infected his students with his hostility to Nominalist theology, and in October, 1516, he was coaching for the master's examinations six or seven candidates through whom he promised "to bring Aristotle to disgrace." Already he had taken the field through one of his students. Bartholomew Bernhardi, a Wittenberg master, was to be advanced to sententiarius in September of that year, and a public disputation was staged when the candidate defended a number of theses on the "powers and will of man without grace." [39] These propositions represented man as absolutely incapable by his own efforts of keeping the commands of God, and arraigned the ruling scholastic theory as stained with Pelagian heresy. For the first time Luther's ideas thus became the subject of a public dissertation. He himself presided and was delighted at the effect on the "Gabrielists," as he calls the defenders of scholastic theory in Wittenberg and Erfurt.[40]

A year later academic circles were again agitated by another similar public disputation, where one of Luther's candidates for the Bible baccalaureate, Franz Gunther, September 4, 1517, defended ninety-

---

[38] *Enders*, I, 59.
[39] *"Quaestio de viribus et voluntate hominis sine gratia"* (*WA*, I, 142ff.).
[40] Letter to Lang, Sept., 1516 (*Enders*, I, 55).

nine theses, which are an echo of his professor's teaching against scholastic doctrines of natural goodness, with sharp comments on the destructive influence of Aristotle on theology.[41] Gunther's theses contain already, in *petto*, Luther's whole formulation of the nature of Christianity. They direct a bold frontal attack on scholastic theology. They array Augustine against Aristotle and religion against morality. They hurl open defiance at William of Occam and his theological system. They proclaim a thorough distrust of natural man and his merits and they extol grace as that which saves from the despair and discouragement of the law by filling men with the conception of Christian liberty. These were ideas to which, as we have seen, Luther had found his way in the lectures on Romans. Now through one of his students he proclaims them with the vigor and assurance of a victor.

Less than three months later the ardent will, which was fired with these convictions like wood by red-hot iron (a favorite image of Luther's),[42] showed that it was no longer to be restrained by the academic field. The monk was now ready to emerge as a public character; the professor to become a leader outside of academic walls. The urge to spread his views made him cultivate contacts far and wide by correspon-

[41] *"Disputatio contra scholasticam theologiam"* (*WA*, I, 224ff.).
[42] Cf. disputation of 1520 (*WA*, VI, 94, 10ff.).

dence and turn to his native tongue, which as a scholar and humanistic philologian he had thus far hardly judged a proper medium for theological subjects. The impulse to interpret the doctrine of faith and grace to such an audience as gathered before him in the Wittenberg parish church had early in 1517 driven him to write down his first German work, an interpretation of the seven penitential psalms. It is couched in a German that is, to be sure, queer and stiff, but gives evidence of the imaginative and forceful diction which was to reach such full development three years later.

From the end of 1516 Luther's convictions as to the path on which grace comes to man had become so powerful and explosive that it was only a question of time when he must seek a larger arena to proclaim them than mendicant order or university afforded. No one could have predicted that within two years this arena would also contain the highest officials of the Roman Church and the German Empire or that the name of the mendicant monk-professor would have found its way into the correspondence of the highest chancelleries of Europe. Least of all did Luther himself anticipate such a result when at the end of October, 1517, he prepared his theses against indulgences. "I was completely dead to the world," he says, looking back upon those stirring days many years later, "until God believed the time had come. Then

Junker Tetzel excited me with indulgences and Doctor Staupitz spurred me on against the Pope." The remark is characteristic and one of many which indicate that at the very moment when he attempted the boldest undertakings he moved under the impulse of a powerful fatalism. "The sons of God are acted upon, rather than themselves actors," he had declared in one of his earliest polemics.[43]

The powerful, subconscious forces which led him to repeat for himself the question which Anselm had asked four centuries earlier, "Why God, man?" ("*Cur deus, homo?*") to repeat it with ever increasing intensity until he had found a solution, drove him along unhaltingly to draw the consequences of his faith in powerful action. Occasionally in the months following the great protest of October, 1517, he looked around him with something like consternation at the uproar aroused by his theses. "If the boldness and ignorance of these people had not been so great," [44] he wrote to his bishop after the promulgation of the *Ninety-five Theses,* "no one would ever have known me outside of my corner." As a matter of fact the opening of a fight against indulgences was the next inevitable step for a man filled with the conception of justification which Luther had acquired and fired by an impulse to redirect what he believed to be the erring theology of his time. Among the

[43] *WA,* I, 649, 28; cf. *Enders,* II, 323, 28.
[44] Letter of Feb. 13, 1518.

whole body of ecclesiastical abuses on which his eyes had fixed since he had become a doctor of theology, circumstances brought this particular one just at this time immediately and inescapably before his vision. His whole dearly bought theory of justification and of man's attitude toward sin and grace demanded that he express himself. A man who had been "attacked by God" and who had felt from the beginning the realism and actuality of sin could not pause in the face of a travesty on forgiveness. Two or three years before, in an early sermon, he had drawn a striking contrast between the repentance that hates God's justice and the true repentance that loves God and hates sin.

In striding to action the monk-professor took the only path known to him for finding the formulas of truth, the academic disputation, this time not under cover of his students but through theses defended by himself. The *Ninety-five Theses* are a natural corollary to the lectures on Romans and on Galatians. Opening with a differentiation between the inner, life-long repentance demanded by Christ and the outer, ecclesiastical order of sacraments, they show how the moral change which Christ demands differs from the punishments demanded by the Church. The expansion and variation of this theme in a powerfully imaginative style which strains at the leash of its academic Latin leads finally to the mystical plea which rings so often in the lectures on Romans, the plea for a recognition of the true value of suffering as a gateway to heaven.[45]

The circle of thought is now complete. The development which led from the conviction of the reality of sin through the consolations of Gerson and Bernard to the God-intoxication of Augustine and the self-surrender of the Mystical Fathers had now brought the seeker to Saint Paul and a God of Love. The mystery of grace has become for him an intense and ever-repeated experience of healing and salvation.

---

[45] *WA*, I, 99ff. It was just about this time, 1517, that Luther expresses the idea of joy through suffering in the verse on his seal:

> *Des Christen Herz auf Rosen geht*
> *Auch wenn es unterm Kreuze steht.*

> (The Christian rests on beds of flowers,
> Even though the cross above him towers.)

Cf. Ficker, *Luther, 1917*, 10, 36.

INDEX *

* The index contains only important names and works mentioned in the text.

229